Journey to the Sacred Mountains

ABOUT THE AUTHOR

Flynn Johnson is the founder of The School of Natural Wonder, which has been offering Vision Quests and other Earth-centered programs for adolescents and adults since 1993.

He also has a shamanic healing practice. To visit his website go to *www.questvision.org*. He lives in Vermont with his wife and son.

Journey to the Sacred Mountains

Awakening Your Soul in Nature

Flynn Johnson

FINDHORN PRESS

The right of Flynn Johnson to be
identified as the author of this work has been asserted by him
in accordance with the Copyright, Designs and Patents Act 1998.

Published in 2010 by Findhorn Press, Scotland

ISBN 978-1-84409-512-4

Edited by Nicky Leach
Cover design by Richard Crookes
Interior design by Damian Keenan
Printed and bound in the USA

1 2 3 4 5 6 7 8 9 17 16 15 14 13 12 11 10

Published by
Findhorn Press
117-121 High Street,
Forres IV36 1AB,
Scotland, UK

t +44 (0)1309 690582
f +44 (0)131 777 2711
e info@findhornpress.com
www.findhornpress.com

Contents

Journey to the Sacred Mountains

I entered the life of the brown forest,
And the great life of the ancient peaks, the patience of stone,
I felt the changes in the veins
In the throat of the mountain,
and I was the stream,

Draining the mountain wood; and I the stag drinking:
and I was the stars,

Boiling with light, wandering alone,
each one the lord of his own summit;
and I was the darkness

Outside the stars, I included them. They were part of me.
I was mankind also, a moving lichen

On the cheek of the round stone… they have not made words for it…
                    — THE TOWER BEYOND TRAGEDY, ROBINSON JEFFERS

Acknowledgments

I gratefully acknowledge my wife, Jill Gia Neitlich, for her unwavering love and belief in me. She has been and continues to be a rich source of inspiration and ideas for me.

To my brother, who died too young, I acknowledge your beautiful heart and love of the wild. To my father, I gratefully acknowledge your poet's love of the moon and pray that your pain has come to an end. To my mother, I am grateful for the undying love and support you gave me, even when I turned my back on you.

I am grateful to the muse who visited me in my dream and gave me the boost to enter into the uncharted waters of writing this book.

I am grateful to all the participants on our Vision Quest programs, who have inspired me with their courage and wisdom.

I am grateful to Tom Wilkins, my brother's dear friend, who invited me to support him at a Sun Dance and who dances the Medicine Way with integrity and heart.

I give thanks to my editor, Sabine Weeke, for her interest and enthusiasm for this book; and to Nicky Leach for her insightful editorial suggestions and for her heartfelt praise for this book. I am very grateful to my dear friends who read the manuscript early on, gave me encouragement, and said what they thought: Alan Steinberg, Fred Taylor, Miriam Dror, Charlie Laurel, Lindsay Cobb, and Suzanne Kingsbury.

I am indebted to my many teachers and mentors, both here and beyond, especially the late Steven Foster and Meredith Little, who modeled the wild heart and fervent imagination needed to live on the threshold.

I am grateful for the vision of the American Indians that stays true to the winds of Great Spirit and to the care for all our relations.

Introduction

I invite you to join me around the fire circle. We are about to take a journey of the imagination into the dynamics of spiritual transformation as revealed in a profound and fiercely beautiful Plains Indian story, The Story of Jumping Mouse. Through powerful images drawn from Nature, this story portrays the journey to awareness as one that is forged through a deepened relationship with self, others, and the natural world. At its core, the story teaches the way of the Vision Quest as a vehicle for realizing a deepened relationship with Spirit.

The Vision Quest is an American Indian initiation ceremony designed to clearly mark, honor, and celebrate the passage from childhood to adulthood. Among the Plains Indians, a young person is placed out on a hill where, while fasting for four days and nights, he "cries for a vision" of who he is and what gifts he has to give to his people. Through the Quest, he realizes his unique relationship to Spirit, which becomes the foundation for his life as an adult.

So, please join me in the circle. Right now I am holding the talking stick and preparing the ground for the telling of this story, and then commenting on it. When you hold the talking stick, you speak from the heart and those listening listen from the heart. Coming from the heart, the words we speak can touch us, and we can touch each other. In this way, our circle is held strong, and we are joined as brothers and sisters on our Earth Walk.

Stories are gifts from the ancient ones who walked this land before us. They tell us who and what we are as human beings. They tell us what is of value and how to love each other and all life forms that share this beautiful Earth with us. Stories speak of beginnings and of the road of aspiration and beauty. If they are like this one—and not all stories are—they use images that stir the longing for awakening within our hearts.

This story teaches an ancient indigenous way of perceiving and being in the world. It teaches that all the faces of Nature—from its creatures to its elemental powers—are interconnected in a vast web of relational intimacy, interdependence, and reciprocity.

In his epic masterpiece Seven Arrows, the mixed blood, enrolled Indian Hyemeyohsts (Hi-yuyh-may-yoh-sts) Storm calls this intimate bond among all beings "touching." True seeing arises out of this touching; it is a communion between self and Other. In this touching, both seer and seen are revealed as imbued with soul and spirit. In this native way of seeing, humans and the natural world mirror each other.

I recount and offer commentary on this story with great respect for the Plains Indians and their vision, into which, as a white man, I can only partially enter. My intention is that this story will speak to you as it has to me. I hope that it will elicit a response from your heart that will move outward in ever-expanding rings of interconnection. In this way, our many hearts may sing as one and together we can create ways of being on this sacred Earth that stand as alternatives to our modern estrangement from each other and Nature.

* * *

Before I begin the story and commentary, I want to tell you about the origins of this book in the fields of my own life and the work from which it has grown.

It was through my work as a wilderness Vision Quest guide that the story really took hold. It grew within me, both personally and professionally, as I told it countless times over the course of 15 years to hundreds of people the night before they set out on a Vision Quest.

I came to being a Vision Quest guide through my work as a psychological counselor at a college. One day, the outdoor program director asked me if I'd like to lead one of the woods orientation trips that are offered to incoming students. I liked the idea. As these students stood at the threshold of entering a whole new world at college, it seemed like a perfect opportunity to enact a contemporary version of this ancient rite of passage ceremony. So I created a rite of passage experience, based on my studies in this area and my own personal Vision Quests. The first trip was a success, and I enjoyed the experience so much that I decided to do a wilderness Vision Quest guide training with Meredith Little and the late Steven Foster, pioneers in developing modern wilderness rites of passage.

The training involved participating as an apprentice in a youth Vision Quest program for nine young people, ranging in age from 15 to 21. Before the young people arrived, we received instructions in the dynamics of rites of passage, a Medicine Wheel, the art of mirroring, and much more. When the participants arrived, we witnessed Steven and Meredith skillfully and lovingly prepare and guide them through the Vision Quest experience. What left the deepest and most abiding impression upon me was the love and respect they gave to these young people. I saw how their loving acceptance gave each person the safety and freedom to reveal what was really going on in his or her life—the pain, fears, questions, doubts, longings, and joys.

This training was a very powerful experience for me, both personally and professionally. I had asked Steven and Meredith if, in addition to the training, I could also do a Vision Quest, and they had agreed. Consequently, like the young people, I too got a chance to talk in the Elder's Council about my reasons for wanting to undertake a three-day solitary vision fast, and to tell my Vision Quest story when I returned from my solo trip in the wilderness. So, in an unplanned way, I was being "initiated" along with these wonderful young people. Even as I write these words more than 10 years later, tears well up in my eyes. Here I was, in midlife, receiving the initiation and elder's blessing that I had unconsciously longed for but never received as a young man.

Sitting in circle each day, as these young people talked about their lives with so much honesty and wisdom, churned up a profound grief from my own adolescence. My adolescence and twenties were a very difficult period in my life. I was in pain and tried to numb it with drugs, alcohol, and women. I was searching for meaning and could not find it anywhere. At times, I stumbled through my days in a fog, a kind of psychic numbing that flattened my emotions and protected me from the simmering rage and shame inside me. I was angry and afraid of what I might do with that anger, so I did what I could to suppress it—not always successfully.

It was only through therapy, many years later, that I began the slow, painful process of unraveling the knots of my pain, anger, and shame.

I traced my suffering back to the alcoholic family system I grew up in. My alcoholic father was an unhappy man. He worked at a job he hated and, as a World War II veteran who had witnessed atrocities, more than likely suffered from undiagnosed post-traumatic stress disorder. He took out his despair and anger on me, the oldest son. In my teens I began to rebel against his tyranny, further driving a wedge between us.

Eventually, I escaped my dysfunctional family by going to college as far away from home as I could get. But, lacking emotional maturity and ambition, I didn't stay the course. I dropped out and got drafted into the army during the height of the Vietnam war. At the time, I really didn't care whether I lived or died. But, through luck or grace, I was sent to Germany instead of Vietnam for my tour.

It was while I was in the army, of all places, that I gradually began to emerge from the fog of my adolescence. I began reading Dostoyevsky and Sartre and started to see my life and suffering through the lens of existentialism. I no longer felt that the questions burning inside me were those of a madman. I no longer felt alone. This was an awakening for me.

At the end of my tour, I returned to college. Soon, I was swept up in the heady furor of the tumultuous counterculture days of the late 1960s. Still rebellious, I dropped out again to join the revolution in the streets. For about eight years I led a vagabond life, hopping freight trains and hitch-hiking all over the United States and Canada, writing poetry and short stories, Kerouac and Nietzsche side by side in my backpack.

My wanderings came to an abrupt halt in 1975 when my younger brother, who operated a tree service, died in a fall from a tree. Numb with grief and despair and trying to make sense of human suffering—indeed, my own suffering—I retreated from life and took up the study of mysticism and philosophy.

Eventually I went to a college in New York City on the G.I. bill so that I could be near my grieving parents, who had descended more deeply into the bottle. Four years later I got an M.A. in philosophy, none the wiser about the meaning of suffering. But even though I was offered a fellowship, I decided not to enroll in the Ph.D program: I found philosophy to be all head and no heart.

Instead, I moved to a vacant ancestral home in the mountains of Vermont to write a novel. This was a beautiful, idyllic place, surrounded by mountains and meadows, where I had spent many a happy summer as a child. Here I lived a semi-hermetic life, driving a school bus, writing a novel, and meditating a few hours each day.

The beauty that was all around me and regular meditation did much to heal the pain I'd been carrying inside for many years. In fact, I think it saved my life. But after seven years of this I realized that I no longer wanted to live the life of a monk, so I left the mountains and reentered the world.

A big part of my reentry involved seeking a better understanding of my suffering through therapy and getting involved with a woman I had known during my wandering years, whom I eventually married. Also at this time, I returned to school to get a M.A. degree in Counseling Psychology. Like a recent convert, I fervently believed that psychotherapy held the key to unlock people's suffering. Eventually, I got a position as a counselor at a college, where I hoped to help young people who were wandering in the dark woods, as I had done.

This thumbnail sketch of my life brings us back to the training in the foothills of California's Sierra Nevada. As I sat in circle listening and feeling, I felt a sweet healing taking place. I saw my adolescent self reflected in the stories and feelings expressed by these young people. As my heart went out to them, it circled back and embraced with acceptance the pain and longings of my adolescent self.

I was able to honor him in a way that I had never been able to do before, and I was able to see how my wounds and longings had shaped my soul and character in a fruitful way. For one thing, it allowed me to feel compassion for these young people. This was another major turning point in my life.

My Vision Quest experience itself reinforced the transformation that I was undergoing. On the last night, I stayed up all night inside a circle of stones, shaking a rattle, dancing, and singing to the full moon, which floated above the high desert like a celestial companion. A song rose up out of my bones and circled Grandmother Moon with wings of joy. I sang most of the night and was transported by song into another reality.

Then, as dawn began to spread slowly and tenderly over the sage flats below me, a hawk swooped down out of nowhere within a few feet of my head. The sheer suddenness and explosiveness of its flight took my breath away. I dropped to my knees and gave thanks for the beauty and mystery of this winged blessing. I felt that Great Spirit had affirmed the path that was leading me into being a Vision Quest guide.

A year or so after this training I left the college to found The School of Natural Wonder, which is dedicated to helping individuals connect more deeply with themselves, each other, and the natural world by means of the Vision Quest process and other Earth-based programs.

After almost a decade of guiding people to the Sacred Mountains, the idea for this book came to me, but I hesitated in beginning the project because Steven and Meredith had already used The Story of Jumping Mouse skillfully in their book *The Roaring of the Sacred River: The Wilderness Quest for Vision and Self-Healing*. I just couldn't let go of the idea, though, and while on a personal Vision Quest, I had a dream that seemed to urge me to go ahead with the book.

In the dream, I heard a voice instruct me to pay attention to The Frog Sutra. Before I had gone out on this Vision Quest, a working title that I had given to the book was *Do You Want Some Medicine Power?* These are words spoken by the character Frog twice in the story.

Now a sutra is a narrative based on a discourse by the Buddha or a Hindu doctrinal teaching. Not to leave any stone unturned, I did some research to see if there actually was a Frog Sutra. I couldn't find any reference to a sutra of that title. So I concluded that the dream was instructing me to begin working with the teachings that Frog had to offer in the Jumping Mouse story.

This instruction, of course, could be interpreted in two ways:

First, it could have to do with my own quest and relationship to medicine power. Second, it could have to do with coming to a deeper understanding of the teachings of Frog for the sake of the book that I was thinking about writing.

The way things turned out is that both of these possibilities have merged through the writing process. Writing this book has both greatly deepened my understanding of the Medicine Power that Frog offers Little Mouse in the story and at the same time, circling back, has thrown into bold relief the direction of my own spiritual path.

The most important lesson that Frog teaches Little Mouse is that he must first humble himself if he is to discover his Medicine Power. He teaches him that he must let go of his self-centeredness and self-importance in order to reach his highest spiritual potential. In short, he teaches him to follow the urgings of Spirit, instead of the desires of ego.

As Little Mouse surrenders in trust to the winds of Spirit, he acquires the capacity to "see with the eye of the heart" into the heart of another being. This capacity gives him the Medicine Power to respond from the heart to the suffering of another, rather than to deny it or turn away from it out of aversion or indifference.

Through Frog's teachings, Little Mouse learns that his own quest for self-discovery and self-healing is inseparable from his capacity to act selflessly for the well-being of others. This is virtually a universal teaching to be found in the major religions of the world, especially in Christ's root teachings and the way of the Bodhisattva in Mayahana Buddhism.

It is this orientation to suffering—my own and that of the world—that has taken root in my own heart more strongly as I have followed Jumping Mouse on his journey toward transformation. Having emerged from an alcoholic family system burdened with anger, shame, and a fear of life, I have been on a long journey of healing that, in the beginning, found solace in Nature and later a "pathless path" through the Vision Quest.

The Vision Quest strips you down to nothing, and, as you stand naked before the fierce fires of self-revelation, you are brought face to face paradoxically with both your own vulnerability and greatness of heart. The magic of the quest both humbles and expands you. It teaches you the oneness and equality of all beings, in suffering and joy, and breaks open your heart to receive the whole world.

PART ONE

Separation:

A Glimpse of the
Sacred Mountains

The power that is there for the healing of our world doesn't come from any one of us. As we venture out the power is there. You see, we only need to let the amazing power of self-healing of our planet come through us. And where do we tap into this power?

In our story, in the very journey that we have lived in our lifetime. In our lifetime as Gaia, the planet. This power comes as we drink from the deepest wells of the spirit and hear the song that has been sung through us since time began. The song that burst forth in the forming of the galaxies. The song that sucked biology out of the brimming rocks and that peopled our planet with the exuberance of life forms. This is what sings in us now. And we want it to be kindled, to hear it again stronger. Now that we, in our long planetary journey, have become graced with self-reflexive consciousness, we take glory in those roots and we can let the song sing through us.

—*JOANNA MACY*

The Story of Jumping Mouse

Long ago, or maybe just yesterday, when the Western Prairies were a vast sea of grasses and great herds of shaggy-headed Buffalo flowed across the rolling land like brown rivers and a proud and noble People roamed and lived there beneath an endless blue sky streaked with eagles, a story rose up out of the heart of The People. This story shelters the heart of The People and carries their life-blood, like a sacred bundle, into an unknown future. During long winter nights, storytellers kept The People warm and uplifted with *"The Story of Jumping Mouse."*

Once there was a little mouse.

He was a busy mouse, searching everywhere, touching his whiskers to the grass, and looking. He was busy as mice are—busy with mice things. But once in a while he would hear an odd sound. He would lift his head, squinting hard to see, his whiskers wiggling in the air, and he would wonder. One day he scurried up to a fellow mouse and asked him, "Do you hear a roaring in your ears, my brother?"

"No, no," answered the other mouse, not lifting his busy nose from the ground. "I hear nothing. I am busy now. Talk to me later."

He asked another mouse the same question, and the mouse looked at him strangely. "Are you foolish in your head? What sound?" he asked, and slipped into a hole in a fallen cottonwood tree.

Little Mouse shrugged his whiskers and busied himself again, determined to forget the whole matter. But there was that roaring again. It was faint, very faint, but it was there!

One day, he decided to investigate the sound just a little. Leaving the other busy mice, he scurried a little way away and listened again. There it was! He was listening hard when, suddenly, someone said, "Hello."

21

"Hello, little brother," the voice said, and Little Mouse almost jumped right out of his skin. He arched his back and tail and was about to run.

"Hello," again said the voice. "It is I, Brother Raccoon." And sure enough, it was!

"What are you doing here all by yourself, little brother?" asked the Raccoon. Little Mouse blushed, and put his nose almost to the ground. "I hear a roaring in my ears and I am investigating it," he answered timidly.

"A roaring in your ears?" replied the Raccoon as he sat down with him. "What you hear, little brother, is the river."

"The river?" Little Mouse asked curiously. "What is a river?"

"Walk with me and I will show you the river," Raccoon said.

Little Mouse was terribly afraid, but he was determined to find out once and for all about the roaring. "I can return to my work," he thought, "after this thing is settled, and possibly this thing may aid me in all my busy examining and collecting. And my brothers all said it was nothing. I will show them. I will ask Raccoon to return with me and I will have proof."

"All right, Raccoon, my brother," said Little Mouse. "Lead on to the river. I will walk with you."

Little Mouse walked with Raccoon. His little heart was pounding in his breast. Raccoon was taking him upon strange paths, and Little Mouse smelled the scent of many things that had gone by this way. Many times he became so frightened he almost turned back.

Finally, they came to the river! It was huge and breathtaking, deep and clear in places, and murky in others. Little Mouse was unable to see across it because it was so great. It roared, sang, cried, and thundered on its course. Little Mouse saw great and little pieces of the world carried along on its surface.

"It is powerful!" Little Mouse said, fumbling for words.

"It is a great thing," answered the Raccoon, "but here, let me introduce you to a friend."

In a smoother, shallower place was a lily pad, bright and green. Sitting upon it was a frog, almost as green as the pad it sat on. The frog's white belly stood out clearly.

"Hello, little brother," said the frog. "Welcome to the river."

"I must leave you now," cut in Raccoon, "but do not fear, little brother, for Frog will care for you now." And Raccoon left, looking along the river bank for food that he might wash and eat.

Little Mouse approached the water and looked into it. He saw a frightened mouse reflected there.

"Who are you?" Little Mouse asked. "Are you not afraid, being that far out into the great river?"

"No," answered Frog, "I am not afraid. I have been given the gift from birth to live both above and within the river. When Winter Man comes and freezes this medicine, I cannot be seen. But all the while Thunderbird flies, I am here. To visit me, one must come when the world is green. I, my brother, am the Keeper of the Water."

"Amazing!" Little Mouse said at last, again fumbling for words.

"Would you like to have some medicine power?" Frog asked.

"Medicine power? Me?" asked Little Mouse. "Yes, yes! If it is possible."

"Then crouch as low as you can, and then jump as high as you are able! You will have your medicine!" Frog said.

Little Mouse did as he was instructed. He crouched as low as he could and jumped. And when he did, his eyes saw the Sacred Mountains.

Little Mouse could hardly believe his eyes. But there they were! But then he fell back to Earth, and he landed in the river!

Little Mouse became frightened and scrambled back to the bank. He was wet and frightened nearly to death.

"You have tricked me!" Little Mouse screamed at Frog.

"Wait," said Frog. "You are not harmed. Do not let your fear and anger blind you. What did you see?"

"I," Mouse stammered, "I, I saw the Sacred Mountains!"

"And you have a new name!" Frog said. "It is Jumping Mouse."

"Thank you. Thank you," Jumping Mouse said, and thanked him again. "I want to return to my people and tell them of this thing that has happened to me."

"Go. Go then," Frog said. "Return to your people. It is easy to find them. Keep the sound of the Medicine River to the back of your head. Go opposite to the sound and you will find your brother mice."

Jumping Mouse returned to the world of the mice. But he found disappointment. No one would listen to him. And because he was wet and had no way of explaining it because there had been no rain, many of the other mice were afraid of him. They believed he had been spat from the mouth of another animal that had tried to eat him. And they all knew that if he had not been food for the one who wanted him, then he must also be poison for them.

Jumping Mouse lived again among his people, but he could not forget his vision of the Sacred Mountains.

The memory burned in the mind and heart of Jumping Mouse, and one day he went to the edge of the River Place...

Jumping Mouse went to the edge of the Place of Mice and looked out onto the Prairie. He looked up for eagles. The sky was full of many spots, each one an eagle. But he was determined to go to the Sacred Mountains. He gathered all of his courage and ran just as fast as he could onto the Prairie. His little heart pounded with excitement and fear.

He ran until he came to a stand of sage. He was resting and trying to catch his breath when he saw an old mouse. The patch of sage Old Mouse lived in was a haven for mice. Seeds were plentiful, and there was nesting material and many things to be busy with.

"Hello," said Old Mouse. "Welcome."

Jumping Mouse was amazed. Such a place and such a mouse! "You are truly a great mouse," Jumping Mouse said, with all the respect he could find. "This is truly a wonderful place. And the eagles cannot see you here, either," Jumping Mouse said.

"Yes," said Old Mouse, "and one can see all the beings of the Prairie here: Buffalo, Antelope, Rabbit, and Coyote. One can see them all from here and know their names."

"That is marvelous," Jumping Mouse said. "Can you also see the river and the Great Mountains?"

"Yes and no," Old Mouse said with conviction. "I know there is the Great River. But I am afraid that the Great Mountains are only a myth. Forget your passion to see them and stay here with me. There is everything you want here, and it is a good place to be."

"How can he say such a thing?" thought Jumping Mouse. "The medicine of the Sacred Mountains is nothing one can forget."

"Thank you very much for the meal you have shared with me,

Old Mouse, and also for sharing your great home," Jumping Mouse said. "But I must seek the Sacred Mountains."

"You are a foolish mouse to leave here. There is danger on the Prairie! Look up there!" Old Mouse said, with even more conviction. "See all those spots! They are eagles, and they will catch you!"

It was hard for Jumping Mouse to leave, but he gathered his determination and ran hard again. The ground was rough. But he arched his tail and ran with all his might. He could feel the shadows of the spots upon his back as he ran. All those spots! Finally he ran into a stand of chokecherries. Jumping Mouse could hardly believe his eyes. It was cool there and very spacious. There was water, cherries and seeds to eat, grasses to gather for nests, holes to be explored, and many, many other busy things to do. And there were a great many things to gather.

He was investigating his new domain when he heard very heavy breathing. He quickly investigated the sound and discovered its source. It was a great mound of hair with black horns. It was a great buffalo. Jumping Mouse could hardly believe the greatness of the being he saw lying there before him. He was so large that Jumping Mouse could have crawled into one of his great horns. "Such a magnificent being," thought Jumping Mouse, and he crept closer.

"Hello, my brother," said Jumping Mouse. "Why are you lying here?"

"I am sick and dying," Buffalo said, "And my medicine has told me that only the eye of a mouse can heal me. But little brother, there is no such thing as a mouse."

Jumping Mouse was shocked. "One of my eyes!" he thought. "One of my tiny eyes." He scurried back into the stand of chokecherries. But the breathing came harder and slower.

"He will die," thought Jumping Mouse, "if I do not give him my eye. He is too great a being to let die."

He went back to where Buffalo lay and spoke. "I am a mouse," he said with a shaky voice. "And you, my brother, are a great being. I cannot let you die. I have two eyes, so you may have one of them."

The minute he said it, Jumping Mouse's eye flew out of his head and Buffalo was made whole. Buffalo jumped to his feet, shaking Jumping Mouse's whole world.

"Thank you, my little brother," said Buffalo. "I know of your quest for the Sacred Mountains and of your visit to the river. You have given me life so that I may Give-Away to The People. I will be your brother forever. Run under my belly, and I will take you right to the foot of the Sacred Mountains, and you need not fear the spots. The eagles cannot see you while you run under me. All they will see will be the back of a buffalo. I am of the Prairie, and I will fall on you if I try to go up the mountains."

Little Mouse ran under Buffalo, secure and hidden from the spots, but with only one eye it was frightening. The buffalo's great hooves shook the whole world each time he took a step.

Finally they came to a place where Buffalo stopped.

"This is where I must leave you, little brother," said Buffalo.

"Thank you very much," said Jumping Mouse. "But you know, it was very frightening running under you with only one eye. I was constantly in fear of your great earth-shaking hooves."

"Your fear was for nothing," said Buffalo. "For my way of walking is the Sun Dance way, and I always know where my hooves will fall. I now must return to the Prairie, my brother. You can always find me there."

Jumping Mouse immediately began to investigate his new surroundings. There were even more things here than in the other places—busier things, and an abundance of seeds and other things mice like. In his investigation of these things, suddenly he ran upon a gray wolf who was sitting there doing absolutely nothing.

"Hello, Brother Wolf," Jumping Mouse said.

Wolf's ears came alert and his eyes shone. "Wolf?! Wolf?! Yes, that is what I am. I am a wolf!" But then his mind dimmed again, and it was not long before he sat quietly again, completely without memory as to who he was. Each time Jumping Mouse reminded him who he was, he became excited with the news, but soon would forget again.

"Such a great being," thought Jumping Mouse, "but he has no memory."

Jumping Mouse went to the center of this new place and was quiet. He listened for a very long time to the beating of his heart. Then suddenly he made up his mind. He scurried back to where the wolf sat and he spoke.

"Brother Wolf," Jumping Mouse said.

"Wolf?! Wolf?!" said Wolf.

"Please listen to me. I know what will heal you. It is one of my eyes. And I want to give it to you. You are a greater being than I. I am only a mouse. Please take it."

When Jumping Mouse stopped speaking his eye flew out of his head and Wolf was made whole.

Tears fell down the cheeks of Wolf, but his little brother could not see them, for now he was blind.

"You are a great brother," said Wolf, "for now I have my memory. But now you are blind. I am the guide into the Sacred Mountains. I will take you there. There is a Great Medicine Lake there—the most beautiful lake in the world. All the world is reflected there. The People, the lodges of The People, and all the beings of the Prairies and Skies."

"Please take me there," Jumping Mouse said.

Wolf guided him through the pines to the Medicine Lake. Jumping Mouse drank the water from the lake. Wolf described the beauty to him.

"I must leave you here," said Wolf, "for I must return so that I may guide others, but I will remain with you as long as you like."

"Thank you, my brother," said Jumping Mouse. "But although I am frightened to be alone, I know you must go so that you may show others the way to this place."

Jumping Mouse sat there trembling in fear. It was no use running, for he was blind, he knew an eagle would find him here. He felt a shadow on his back and heard the sound that eagles make. He braced himself for the shock. And the eagle hit! Jumping Mouse went to sleep.

Then he woke up. The surprise of being alive was great, but now he could see! Everything was blurry, but the colors were beautiful.

"I can see! I can see!" said Jumping Mouse over again and again.

A blurry shape came toward Jumping Mouse. Jumping Mouse squinted hard, but the shape remained a blur.

"Hello, brother," a voice said. "Do you want some medicine?"

"Some medicine for me?" asked Jumping Mouse. "Yes! Yes!"

"Then crouch down as low as you can," the voice said, "and jump as high as you can."

Jumping Mouse did as he was instructed. He crouched as low as he could and jumped! The wind caught him and carried him higher.

"Do not be afraid," the voice called to him. "Hang on to the wind and trust!"

Jumping Mouse did. He closed his eyes and hung on to the wind and it carried him higher and higher. Jumping Mouse opened his eyes, and they were clear, and the higher he went the clearer they became. Jumping Mouse saw his old friend upon a lily pad on the beautiful Medicine Lake. It was Frog.

"You have a new name," called Frog. "You are Eagle!"

The Call of
the Unknown

*The Vision Quest, or perceiving quest, is the way we must begin this
search. We must all follow our Vision Quest to discover ourselves, to
learn how we perceive of ourselves, and to find our relationship with
the world around us.*

—*HYEMEYOHSTS STORM*

The main character of our story is a mouse. He is just one mouse among many
other mice, without even a name. Each of us begins life in a somewhat similar
place. We are born into a body, immersed in a family and a larger collective body, and
ignorant of our true name—our true nature. The story of this particular mouse unfolds
as a quest to discover his true nature. To do this, however, he must first free himself
from his unconscious submergence in the mindset of the collective body. In the native
understanding of the soul's journey, he must begin to explore and integrate the powers of the four sacred directions of the Medicine Wheel, the wheel representing the
Universe and its myriad life forms as an interdependent whole.

In the absence of a name, the mouse is described as just a "little mouse." His little-
ness stands out as an important detail. Little Mouse is little in two interrelated ways.
On the one hand, he is little relative to the vastness of the world that surrounds him,
a world of which he knows so little; on the other hand, he is little in relation to the
unknown potential that lies within him, like a seed awaiting the right conditions to
grow. The vastness of these two unknown dimensions of his life mirror each other and
frame the life of Little Mouse.

In this regard, the story mirrors the human soul's journey, expressing a paradox
intrinsic to our existential situation. On the one hand, it speaks of our humble place
in a vast Universe that reaches far back into the beginnings of life and stretches ahead
into an unknown future. It hints at the vast mystery that we find ourselves immersed
in, the mystery of life itself—the miracle that there is something rather than nothing.
On the other hand, the story calls to us to stretch ourselves beyond the small world

that we know so well into the unknown possibilities of human consciousness. In this way, at the very beginning the story begins to weave together the inner and outer mystery that frame our Earth Walk.

The opening of the story finds Little Mouse "busy with mice things." Like all the other mice, he is busy gathering and collecting seeds and nuts for the sake of his survival, for when you live off the land you must always be prepared for the harshness of winter. Rooted in a land-based indigenous culture, the story points to the reality that the basic needs of the body for food, clothing, and shelter must be met first before there is time for any other considerations. In spite of these material demands, however, anthropological studies show that indigenous peoples had more leisure time for socializing, play, and ritual than we moderns. Even so, the story warns the native listener of the danger of becoming overly caught up in the material concerns of life, at the expense of one's spiritual life.

It is interesting that even in a tribal world the tendency toward busyness was a feature of that life. Perhaps this tendency is common to the human experience, regardless of time and culture.

The busyness of a tribal life, however, clearly pales in comparison to the reality of our fast-paced, modern, industrialized world. In many ways, busyness is a defining feature of our lives as we rush about from here to there in the midst of our own struggles for security and comfort. Our days are packed full with commutes to and from work, appointments, phone calls to make, e-mails to check and send, deadlines, planes to catch, children to taxi from here to there, and on and on, with little or no time to stop and observe what is actually going around us, let alone inside us.

We move through life so fast we can forget to really see, hear, smell, taste, or touch anything. As a result, our senses can become impoverished or even shut down. This is especially true if we live in an urban environment where we must shield ourselves from sensory overload.

But our senses are the windows of our bodies through which a vibrant, sensual, ensouled world enters—through which the many faces of Spirit approach us. Our senses form the invisible threads that connect us with life and whatever is other than ourselves. Ironically, even though our cultural orientation to reality is predominately materialistic, we have somehow left our bodies behind, except as idealized expressions of physical beauty or prowess. In the end, our weakened connections to a vibrant world and the stresses of our fast-paced lifestyle take a toll not only on our bodies but also on our souls.

In this regard, the observations of someone who has lived outside our culture, especially those of an indigenous person, can be revealing.

Malidoma Somé is a medicine man in the Dagara culture of West Africa who holds multiple graduate degrees from Western universities. In *Ritual: Power, Healing and Community*, he observes that when an indigenous person comes to the West for the first time what shocks him most is the *speed* at which our mechanized, industrialized world operates. As he insightfully notes, the speed of our society is not a movement toward something, but rather a flight *away from* something. It is a flight away from any real contact with the deeper stirrings of our inner life and with each other. Somé describes the psychic and spiritual impact of the speed of our culture when he discusses the difference between our mechanized world and indigenous life.

> Indigenous people are indigenous because there are no machines between them and their gods. There are no machines barring the door to the spirit world where one can enter in and listen to what is going on within at a deep level, participating in the vibration of Nature.
>
> Where machines speak in place of gods, people are hard put to listen, even more hard put to vibrate with the realm of Nature… Such a life eats at the psyche and moves its victims faster and faster along, as they are progressively emptied out of their spiritual and psychic fuel. It is here, consequently, where one's spirit is in crisis, that speed is the yardstick by which the crisis itself is expressed.

As Somé suggests, the frenetic speed of our culture and the corresponding flight away from ourselves are signs of a spiritual crisis. On the one hand, this spiritual crisis is marked by a pervasive and disturbing estrangement from our inner life—both our emotional life (our emotional body) and our deep intuitive knowing that flows beneath the surface of our rational minds.

As we rush about from here to there, driven by a cultural obsession with consumption, wealth, fame, and personality, we are in danger of becoming soulless automatons who are influenced and motivated more by superficial outer forces and values than by any inner sense of direction and rightness. In the absence of an engaged inner life, we lose our moral compass and the depth of soul that goes to make up genuine character. In addition, we have difficulty accessing the deeper emotional currents within us and, as a consequence, our relationships can suffer from an enervating shallowness. In the midst of material security (for some), our souls are languishing and crying out.

At the same time, this spiritual crisis reveals itself in an equally profound and disturbing estrangement from the natural world. The road to modernity, paved by a rational, scientific worldview, has severed our original connection to a vibrant, animated, ensouled world. We have been separated from our original home in Nature.

In many ways, this spiritual crisis may be understood as an alienation from our own indigenous soul—the primal, intuitive, embodied part of humanity that lived for many thousands of years in an immediate and intimate connection with the rhythms and beings of the natural world and that still resides within our genetic and spiritual makeup just beneath the thin masks of civilization. It is the part of ourselves that once felt at home on Earth, and that longs to revive that lost connection.

A Roaring in the Ears

All is not lost, though, for like Little Mouse, we have not lost the capacity to slow down and listen. And when we do, we may also hear a roaring in our ears that stirs our memory and wonder, and provokes an investigation into its source.

In the midst of Little Mouse's busyness, he would occasionally hear an "odd sound" that would cause him to stop whatever he was doing and listen. As he listened, he would "wonder."

Who among us has not had a similar moment—a moment when our attention is arrested by an occurrence that interrupts our ceaseless movement from one thing to another? It could be a full moon floating on the rim of a hill, a small flower emerging from beneath the retreating winter snow, a look in our lover's eyes, the face of a small child, or the difficult times when we experience the shock of the death of a loved one or the ending of a friendship or a marriage.

In such moments our minds quiet down, and we sink fully into the present moment. In such moments wonder settles upon our hearts, like a bird landing on a branch. Wonder opens a door to the Infinite. With wonder comes the possibility for something new to enter our lives, and thus for the possibility of change. Wonder can also stimulate curiosity about the world and a questioning into the preexisting order of things.

We can also quiet our minds through a spiritual practice of one kind or another. For instance, within Buddhism, the practice of meditation is a method for quieting down the incessant internal chatter of our ordinary minds, which is likened to a waterfall or a monkey. Like a monkey, our minds jump from one topic to another without pause, often without rhyme or reason.

In many ways, the busyness of our everyday lives and the incessant busyness of our minds mirror each other: each represents a flight from our true nature. Meditation, in part, seeks to observe the mind from a place of nonattachment to this constantly shifting stream of thoughts and emotions. Through this process, we can discover the true nature of mind in its intrinsic stillness, clarity, and openness.

By noticing the roaring sound and inquiring about its origin, Little Mouse in our story is learning to slow down and pay attention. But the other mice are far too caught up in their own struggle for existence to pay heed to his inquiries about the source of the roaring noise. One mouse even looks at him like he is crazy. Indeed, anyone who introduces something new into the routines and certainties of the collective runs the risk of being judged harshly and in some cases being ostracized or even killed. Chances are, however, that some of the other mice also hear a roaring in their ears but *choose* to deny it, fearing that it might somehow threaten their fragile security and cherished habits. It is seemingly much safer to conform than to risk stepping into the unknown.

Little Mouse also tries to put the roaring out of his mind by busying himself again, but he just can't do it. He continues to hear it, ever so faintly in the back of his awareness, like the hum of a forest at dusk. So one day he scurries a little way from the other mice to investigate.

As he's listening, he is suddenly frightened nearly out of his skin by Brother Raccoon, who asks him what he's doing so far away from his people. Overcoming his embarrassment, Little Mouse tells him he is investigating a roaring in his ears. Raccoon tells him that the roaring is the river. Well, Little Mouse has never seen a river, so Raccoon offers to take him there. Understandably, Little Mouse is very frightened by the prospect of venturing forth from familiar territory into the unknown. However, thinking that knowledge of the river might be of some practical value for his fellow mice, he agrees to go with Raccoon.

When they arrive at the river, Little Mouse is truly amazed at its greatness. His sense of wonder before the river quickly displaces his initial pragmatic intention. But what is this Great River that "roared, sang, cried, and thundered on its course?"

The Great River sings the Song of Life that awakens our hearts from the slumber of taking things for granted and forgetfulness. The Great River roars in our blood with the quickened pulse and wild energy of life, pushing our borders into the borderless terrain of the unknown. The lifeblood of Mother Earth thunders in the river and demands to be heard. To ignore it is to risk a death while living; it is to renounce being fully alive for the sake of security and comfort. To hear it and embrace it is to dance with life and death in the ecstatic moment. The river is the source of all life, the infinite vital energy of the Universe streaming through its billions of manifestations; it is Life itself, calling us forth beyond the known into a more abundant expression of itself.

To his inestimable credit, Little Mouse heard and heeded the roaring of life in the deep, hidden sanctuary of his heart. He did not turn a deaf ear to the call issuing forth from the unknown. In the words of the acclaimed mythologist Joseph Campbell, he responded to "the Call to Adventure," which is the first stage in the archetypal Hero's Journey. In brief, the Hero's Journey is a theme found in folktales that describes an individual's journey from ignorance of his true nature to self-awareness.

So, at one level, the roaring in Little Mouse's ear is the cry of our heart's longing for a more abundant, more fulfilled life, which always lies beyond the threshold of our known world. A part of each of us does not want to spend a lifetime with our noses to the ground, not seeing the world beyond the tip of our nose, constantly fearful, and not responding to the fullness of life and to the potential within us. It is life demanding to be lived fully, not half asleep, not in fear, not obsessed with comfort, security, and control, not blinded by a visionless attachment to an exclusively material view of reality.

At another level, as we take the liberty of fast-forwarding to our own time of ecological crisis, the Song of Life has become a cry. The roaring in our ears may also include the cries of Mother Earth and her children, and the cries of the people who are most affected by our mad assault on our own lifeblood.

Our assault on the Earth is well documented scientifically; yet, it seems that many of us remain in denial—especially those in positions of power and privilege who are reaping huge profits at the expense of the Earth, the poor and dispossessed of this country, and the poor countries of the world. As far as we know, Earth is in the midst of the greatest mass extinction since the dinosaurs died off 65 million years ago. Species are disappearing from the face of the Earth at an alarming rate. By 2100, nearly half of all species could be lost forever. And humans are directly responsible for these dire prospects.

We have only to look at how the main characters in our story are faring today to see the impact of our actions. Buffalo, nearly exterminated in the 1800s in a malicious attempt by the U.S. government to destroy the lifeblood of the Plains Indians, is now a mere shadow of his former abundance on the prairie. The namesake of the story, Jumping Mouse, is threatened with extinction, as is Gray Wolf. Frog is now appearing in increasing numbers with deformed legs, and his population is dramatically decreasing and in some cases becoming extinct—phenomena that are thought to correspond to an increasing degree of ecological degradation. The good news is that through protection, Eagle is about to soar off the endangered species list. But will Eagle survive the dying of our lakes and rivers from acid rain, as the fish he feeds on are contaminated by mercury?

So, the roaring that we hear today also speaks of a grief that can appear to be too great to utter, too painful to really feel. This grief swells beneath the rush of our days like a great subterranean river that has been dammed up. It holds the cries of the wildlife dying all around us. It holds our loss of connection to the natural world and our longing to recover this connection.

With this loss of connection we are also experiencing a loss of a part of our human identity, since for many thousands of years humans inhabited Mother Earth just like any other animal in an intimate, interdependent relationship with her. This swollen, unexpressed grief weighs on our hearts, mute and lifeless, draining our spiritual energy. We are afraid to express it for fear we would drown in our tears. We shut off our feelings so that we will not have to feel it. But our grief cries out to be expressed, thunders through our days of stifled despair, roars in our ears under the guise of depression, generalized anxiety, passionless addictions, hyperactivity, indiscriminate anger and violence, suicide, and the dread of being alone and having to look in the mirror of our own soul.

For our sanity we must express it, otherwise we will only know the ground that lies just before us and never truly know the beauty and joy that lies on the other side of our fear-driven busyness. For beauty and joy rise up out of a heart that has descended into the ashes of grief, like the phoenix rising out of its own ashes. Only when we are willing to travel down into the well of grief and longing that give shape and texture to the contours of the heart can we truly be graced by the soaring flight of beauty and joy.

Perhaps we could learn from the indigenous Wirrarika people of Mexico, who make an annual pilgrimage for hundreds of miles from their homes high in the mountains to springs in the desert that they call "the eyes" of Mother Earth. These springs are a sacred place and are seen as the tears of Mother Earth who is weeping for her children. When the Wirrarika arrive they make offerings and prayers, and soon begin weeping themselves as they let go of all the sorrow they've been carrying for the past year. The release of their tears opens their hearts for the next stage of their pilgrimage, which is to the Sacred Mountain rising up out of the desert. Here, they will connect with Spirit and seek to see their lives more clearly, so that they may bring their visions back into their everyday lives.

The following contemporary poem also calls us into the waters of our grief:

The Well of Grief

Those who will not slip beneath
the still surface on the well of grief

turning downward through its black water
to the place where we cannot breathe

will never know the source from which we drink,
the secret water, cold and clear,

nor find in the darkness glimmering
the small round coins

thrown by those who wished for something else.

—*DAVID WHYTE*

Raccoon

Raccoon plays a critical role in Little Mouse's life. Most importantly, he listens to him. He hears his crisis (the roaring in his ears) and validates it as real and worthy of his attention. He does not dismiss or trivialize his wonder, his longing, his questioning—his quest. He does not humiliate him by telling him to forget his longing and to get on with his life, as do many parents and authority figures in response to the pain of the adolescents in their charge. He does not pathologize his seeking as our culture tends to do.

Our culture is blind to the inner, archetypal blueprint that sends young people out on a quest to find their own answers to the big questions: Who am I? What do I have to offer to the world? Where am I going? What is of value? What is real? Instead, in an unconscious disservice to our youth, we tend to treat this very real and necessary search as an aberration. This only adds to their anguish and can push them to the precipice of self-destructive acts. More will be said in the next chapter about the failure of our culture to respond adequately to this archetypal dynamic.

Instead, Raccoon responds by taking Little Mouse directly to the source of the roaring, so that he may experience it firsthand. After they arrive at the river, in response to Little Mouse's amazement at its power, Raccoon simply acknowledges that it is indeed a great thing, places him in the care of Frog, and then waddles away.

Raccoon doesn't launch into a long, complicated explanation about why the river is great. His job is to be a "midwife to the soul" by taking Little Mouse to the source of Life itself, where he can discover its greatness for himself. He takes him to the original teacher, Nature, the River of Life, wonderful and teeming with diversity, wild and cyclical, flowing and dancing, tumultuous and still, beautiful and awesome beyond words. Through direct and immediate experience, Little Mouse will learn about the power of the Great River and the power within himself. The 15th-century Hindu poet Kabir expresses this notion in the following poem:

> *There is nothing but water in the holy pools.*
> *I know, I have been swimming in them.*
> *All the gods sculpted of wood or ivory can't say a word.*
> *I know, I've been crying out to them.*
> *The Sacred Books of the East are nothing but words.*
> *I looked through their covers one day sideways.*

What Kabir talks of is only what he has lived through.
If you haven't lived through something, it is not true.

—*KABIR*

So Raccoon as midwife fulfills the initiatory role of the elders in traditional, indigenous cultures. The elders in these cultures take the initiates away from their families, away from all that is familiar and known, to the initiatory ground in the wilderness of desert, forest, mountain, or jungle. In some of these rites of passage, the elders don masks to highlight the entrance into another dimension of reality, the realm of the ancestors who were present at the beginning of creation and who now dwell in the Otherworld. Thus the mask worn by Raccoon makes him well suited for his role as a guide. Yet in our story it is interesting that as soon as they arrive at the river, Raccoon introduces Little Mouse to Frog, and then saunters off.

Frog

Raccoon guides Little Mouse to the Great River of Life, whose course demarcates the threshold between ordinary and nonordinary reality. Water is universally symbolic of the ever-changing, ever-evolving quality of Life itself. In this regard, water has an ancient association with healing and transformation. For instance, in the ancient Celtic tradition, wells, springs, and rivers were revered as sacred places where the goddesses dwelled. These places were also thought to be portals to the Otherworld. People came from far and wide to drink the healing waters and commune with the spirits that inhabited these places. Water also functions as a medium of transformation within the Christian tradition; here, we need only recall the Biblical source for baptism in Christ's teachings that "unless one is born of water and the Spirit, he cannot enter the kingdom of God."

On the physical plane, the fluidity of water and its capacity to flow around obstacles and to change into different states—fog, rain, and ice—recommends it highly as a symbol of transformation. In addition, water occupies the three planes of the physical world—Earth, Sky, and Underworld—and moves freely between them in a circular pattern. Rain falls from the sky and descends deep into underground springs, which feed rivers and lakes, and then rises up from the Earth as mist and fog, which in turn falls back to the Earth as rain. As Tom Cowan says in *Fire in the Head,* this "circular dynamic ... symbolizes the reconciliation of opposites; since water flows through all arcs of the circle, it unites all polarities." Universally, the symbols of transformation have to do with bringing the polarities that are at war in conventional consciousness—Heaven and Earth, Spirit and Matter, Mind and Body, Good and Evil—into balance and harmony.

At the river, Little Mouse is introduced to Frog, who we learn is Keeper of the Water, the archetypal role of guardian at the threshold between ordinary and nonordinary reality. The metamorphoses that he undergoes on the physical plane, from egg to polliwog to frog, recommend him symbolically as an agent of transformation *par excellence*. Most importantly, however, Frog's Medicine Power resides in his capacity to inhabit two worlds. As Frog says, "I have been given the gift from birth to live both above and within the river."

Symbolically, Frog plays the role of messenger between what is above and what is within, between the visible and the invisible, between ordinary and nonordinary reality, or in psychological language, between consciousness and the unconscious. Like Hermes, the winged messenger of Greek mythology, he is a liminal figure, who has the gift to descend deep into the Underworld, the dark waters of the unconscious, in order to bring to the surface healing medicine. Like shamans among indigenous people from around the world, he possesses the ancient techniques of entering altered states of consciousness at will, during which he travels to the realm of Spirit. Through these journeys he acquires what is needed to heal others. These skills also give him the capacity to guide others to the threshold of the realm of Spirit.

> Little Mouse approached the water and looked into it. He saw a frightened mouse reflected there.
> "Who are you?" Little Mouse asked. "Are you not afraid being that far out into the river?"

Standing on the bank of the river, Little Mouse is understandably afraid in the presence of such powerful medicine; after all, he is standing at the edge of the great mystery of Life itself. And as he looks into the waters he sees his own reflection and asks, "Who are you?" The question that rises up from the depths within him is, Who am I?

According to many spiritual traditions, this is the single most important question one can ask. It is this question that drives the spiritual search for awareness. It is the question that lies at the heart of our longing to connect more deeply with Spirit. It is a question that we can ask ourselves throughout our lives, since the sense of who we are in relation to the world and to Spirit is constantly shifting in the waters of life as experience and awareness grow. It is the question that underlies all other questions.

Next Frog asks Little Mouse the critical question upon which the rest of his days on Earth will hinge. "Would you like to have some Medicine Power?" At first glance, you might think, who wouldn't want power? But the implicit questions are, What are you willing to risk to have Medicine Power and what are you going to do with it once you've got it? If Mouse answers "No," he will go back to the place of the mice and live in ignorance of his true nature, like the other mice. If he answers "Yes," then his life will never be the same again for he will have committed himself to the quest for vision, and he has no way of knowing in advance what that would even look like.

Mouse says "Yes" in an act of surrender to the spirit that moves within him. However, he says "Yes" with a hint of disbelief that someone as small as he is could possibly have Medicine Power.

Sadly, many in our culture share Little Mouse's sense of unworthiness. As a former psychotherapist, I witnessed suffering that usually involved some degree of low self-esteem, which in its most extreme degree presented itself as shame. A person suffering from shame believes that he is an inherently flawed and unworthy human being, someone who must justify his right to exist. In my own personal experience of shame, it infects the psyche as a crippling sense of never being quite good enough, never quite measuring up to some unattainable standard of perfection. As a consequence, it traps us in an unremitting battle against ourselves as we unmercifully hold the sword of judgment over our heads.

In a similar vein, Western Buddhist teachers also find in their work that they must address the issue of self-hatred. It is instructive to note that a few years ago, when some of these teachers raised the issue of self-hatred to the Dalai Lama of Tibet at a conference, he didn't know what they were talking about. Amazingly, self-hatred was an alien concept to him, since it does not exist in his culture. Apparently, thinking of oneself as inherently flawed is not a universal phenomenon but more of a Western one.

Although an analysis of this difference exceeds the scope of this book, two contributing factors leap immediately to the foreground to explain the Tibetan sense of self-esteem.

First, as a culture informed by Buddhism, Tibetans envision the spiritual path as finding one's Buddha Nature, one's inherent basic goodness. Our basic goodness denotes a dawn radiance that exists within each of us behind the clouds of ignorance, pride, anger, hatred, jealousy, and immature desire that normally becloud human consciousness and separate us from each other. And each of us is able to access this radiance in those moments when we penetrate the surface of our self-centered preoccupations and fears with awareness. Seeing human nature as basically good is a radically different worldview than that expressed in the Christian concept of Original Sin, which stigmatizes humanity as fundamentally flawed. Second, despite many of them having been driven from their homeland by the Chinese in 1959, Tibetan people are by nature deeply connected to the land, unlike us in the West. Perhaps more light can be shed on this phenomenon of Western low self-esteem as we explore the nature of the Medicine Power that Frog offers Little Mouse.

Since it is Frog asking the question about Medicine Power, we can assume that it has something to do with the transformative power inherent in his capacity to move freely between ordinary and nonordinary realities. So, somehow this capacity functions as medicine, which at its most fundamental level has to do with healing an illness or a wound.

But what is the illness or wound that Little Mouse suffers from? As indicated above, Little Mouse, like each of us, suffers from the wound of not knowing his true nature. If he can discover the wholeness intrinsic to his true nature, he will be healed and at the same time have Medicine Power, for living from your true nature brings a healing light into a fragmented world.

In a remarkable similarity to the Buddhist view of discovering our "original face" in our Buddha Nature, the Lakota Sioux envision the spiritual path toward wholeness as a quest to "find one's face." This is also known as discovering one's medicine name—the name that reflects an individual's spiritual power, as opposed to the name given to him at birth.

To find one's face in the traditional Lakota way, an individual walks out into Nature, sits naked in a hole with only a buffalo robe for protection from the elements, without food or water, and cries for a vision for four days and nights. Stripped of self-importance, the individual throws himself at the mercy of Great Spirit and prays.

This act of surrender and humility opens the heart to the possibility of receiving a vision of who and what one truly is. One's true nature is revealed through the cultivation of a relationship to Nature as the sacred ground of all life. Arising from that ground is a vision of the gifts one has to give to the community that has nurtured you into life.

Jeanette Armstrong, an Okanagan Indian, beautifully expresses this inseparable bond between an individual, the community, and the land.

> When we say the Okanagan word for ourselves, we are actually saying "the ones who are dream and land together." That is our original identity. Before anything else, we are the living, dreaming Earth pieces.... Another part of the word means that if you take a number of strands of hair, or twine, place them together, and then rub your hands and bind them together, they become one strand... This part of the word refers to us being tied into and part of everything else. It refers to the dream parts of ourselves forming our community... without that deep connection to the environment, to the Earth, to what we actually are, to what humanity is,

we lose our place, and confusion and chaos enter.

In our world today, much confusion and chaos exist, as a consequence of our lost sense of belonging on the Earth. Our psyches and bodies have been torn away from our original home on the Earth, and we are suffering in the void left by this severance.

According to the ecopsychologist Chellis Glendinning, this wound to our psyches has generated symptoms that are similar to those associated with the psychological diagnosis of post-traumatic stress disorder. Estranged from an enlivening relationship with an ensouled natural world and from our own soul, many of us suffer anxiety, hypervigilance, feelings of estrangement from others, a restricted range of affect, depression, and a severely impoverished sense of self. Having either weakly or never formed a bond of attachment to the matrix of Mother Earth, we are left floundering through life, like orphans abandoned in an empty room. The addictive patterns of behavior that are so pervasive in our society—alcohol and drug abuse, eating disorders, promiscuous sexuality, compulsive shopping and television watching, computer games, and so on—are symptomatic of an empty self attempting in vain to fill an inner and outer relational void in unhealthy, self-destructive ways.

We are like the hungry ghosts in Buddhist iconography who, having huge stomachs but small mouths and long, narrow necks, are never able to satisfy their cravings. In the end, our addictions represent our deepest longings run amok—our longings for satisfying relationships with each other, for feeling at home on the Earth, and for a connection to Spirit.

Nature and the human soul mirror one another. As our rational, technological minds strip Nature and anyone associated with her—from indigenous peoples, to poor people, to people of color, to women—of its soul by reducing her to a mere collection of objects or resources for human exploitation and domination, our souls wither and die. As we have de-souled Nature and people other than ourselves, we have simultaneously deadened our own souls.

To compensate for this stripping of soul from the world, we have inflated the importance of the individual, as the archetypal psychologist James Hillman says,

> ...[to] be desirable, attractive, a sex object, or win importance and power. For without these investments in my particular persona, coming from either your subjectivity or my own, *I too am but a dead thing among dead things, potentially forever lonely.*"
> [my own italics]

In a society traumatized by soul loss, increasingly suffering a disconnection from self and others and the consequent erosion of community, the isolated individual is driven to compete ruthlessly with other isolated individuals for the limited tokens of cultural glory, such as wealth, fame, and power.

From a psychological perspective, the wounded ego seeks to compensate for an underlying sense of unworthiness (shame/Original Sin) with a grandiose self-image that is all glitter and no substance. Culturally, the collective ego applauds and rewards a hyper-individualism, which places a greater value on individual rights than on the well-being of the whole. From a mythological perspective, the glorified individual represents the unconscious rebellion of the child against a wrathful Father and the stigma of Original Sin—the revenge of Adam.

Like the narcissistic psychopath, the underbelly of the imperialistic actions of our collective ego is shame-based rage, as we attempt to assert power through control and domination over all that we deem inferior. Empire is the rage of the shamed-based child turned outward. Its power, though extremely destructive of life because of its deadly toys, ultimately springs from an underlying sense of powerlessness. Real power is always life-affirming, as it seeks to build, create, and care for the well-being of the Family of Life.

Although our estrangement from Nature has become extreme in our industrialized world, it would seem that some distance between humans and Nature is a common part of our "felt experience" as beings with self-reflective consciousness. In simple terms, our self-reflective capacity to perceive ourselves as a Subject in relation to an Object inevitably brings with it a degree of distance—of difference—and we may experience this distance as disharmony.

In *Seven Arrows*, Hyemeyohsts Storms points out that humans are unlike animals, which instinctively know of their harmony with life; we must learn it. Even among American Indian cultures, whose spiritual foundation is harmony with Nature, this harmony must still be fully realized through the Vision Quest or other rites of passage, and renewed periodically through ritual to avoid falling away from it. That is precisely what Little Mouse's quest is all about: he is learning his place within the Medicine Wheel, within the harmony of the Circle of Life.

In general, the religious impulse in humanity across all ages and cultures has been to bridge the gap between humanity and Creation as a way of realizing peace and harmony on Earth—our original oneness with all of life. As human beings, we have a choice: either to accentuate the distance and difference out of fear, or to bridge it with Communion and Care. Our dominant cultural orientation is toward the former, to the detriment of both the human and nonhuman worlds.

* * *

So the Medicine Power that Frog offers Little Mouse relates to him finding his true nature by realizing his kinship with the other beings of the world. As Little Mouse will learn on his quest to the Sacred Mountains, self-revelation takes place through a profound encounter with the suffering of the Other. Little Mouse is learning to see through the trance of separateness to the oneness of all beings. He is learning that Medicine Power has to do with realizing one's capacity to bridge the separation between Self and Other that exists within egoic consciousness. He is learning that Medicine Power is equivalent to spiritual power, which universally manifests as a capacity to heal that which has been torn asunder both within oneself and within the world.

> "Medicine Power? Me?" asked Little Mouse.
> "Yes, yes! If it is possible."
> "Then crouch as low as you can, and then jump as high as you are able! You will have your medicine!" Frog said.
> Little Mouse did as he was instructed. He crouched as low as he could and jumped. And when he did, his eyes saw the Sacred Mountains.

In the manner of a skilled guide, Frog instructs Little Mouse to draw on his strengths: his long, strong hind legs. He doesn't tell him to swim across the river, for Little Mouse would certainly fail at that. Building on Little Mouse's strengths, Frog elicits the best in him—sage advice for any mentor working with an adolescent or anyone else in the midst of a spiritual crisis.

But, equally important, in asking Little Mouse to crouch down as low as he can and then jump as high as he is able, Frog is preparing him for the opportunities of self-transformation that lie ahead. He is teaching him, via his body, to humble himself, for only through letting go of his self-centeredness will Little Mouse be able to realize the heights of his spiritual power; that is, only by seeing through the self-centered trance of separateness will Little Mouse be able to see his face in the face of the Other.

Little Mouse does as he is instructed. He takes a leap of faith and sees the Sacred Mountains. But he doesn't see the Sacred Mountains with just his physical eyes; he sees them with the eye of the heart. And he will never be the same, for this glimpse of the shining mountains in the distance has planted a seed of longing in his heart to go there.

After this glimpse of the Sacred Mountains, Little Mouse falls back to Earth, and then tumbles into the river. After a shining vision like that we always fall back to Earth; after an ascent there is always a descent. At this stage in Little Mouse's life, he is too young and inexperienced to integrate a vision of the Sacred Mountains into his daily life. He has much more to learn, much more growing to do, and the best school for that is the Prairie of everyday life. But from now on, his days on Earth will be lived within the circle of a new way of perceiving, for he has had a glimpse of the sacred reality underlying and informing the visible face of life.

A Glimpse of Spirit

Little Mouse may be seen as an adolescent boy or girl who, having had a glimpse of Spirit, must now gain the life experience necessary in order to fully understand and integrate that vision into their daily life. In his book, *He: Understanding Masculine Psychology*, the Jungian psychologist Robert Johnson states that it is fairly common among adolescents to have an experience of what he calls "[their] Christ nature, that is, [their] individuation process, prematurely…" This profound experience, however, is too much for adolescents to handle because it is radically beyond the range of what they have experienced up to this point in their life. Moreover, our culture, for the most part, does not place any value on such an experience, and as a consequence there are few mentors to whom adolescents can bring this experience in order to receive the affirmation and guidance needed.

On a personal note, I had such an experience as a boy of 13, when I had the privilege of spending one month in a summer camp along with 20 or so other members of a Boys Club in the remote woods of New Brunswick, Canada.

One day, while on an expedition to a rustic fishing camp on a river, I was given the task of canoeing back downriver to collect the gear we couldn't carry on the first trip. I was flush with the responsibility given to me, the youngest one in a group of eight. While returning to our camp, I came to a place in the river near a small island that was relatively calm. I stopped paddling to rest. The only sounds I heard were the gentle lapping of the canoe against lily pads and the humming of a million insects in the dense surrounding forest.

As I sat there in the quiet and stillness, I was suddenly overwhelmed with a feeling of awe before the immense majesty and beauty of Nature. Of course, as a young boy, I had no words for this experience. The words I attach to it now as an adult are pale in comparison to the experience itself.

I have no idea how long I sat there. It could have been only a few minutes, or it could have been much longer. I was lost in a timeless dimension of pure ecstatic feeling. When I eventually arrived at camp, I had no one to whom I could recount this experience. There was no way I could tell my peers, for they would have ridiculed me. These were, after all, the boys who had put big rocks in another boy's backpack, and then laughed at him when he cried, struggling up a mountain. Furthermore, I didn't feel close to the two counselors. So this experience, unexpressed and not validated, lay dormant within me. However, retrospectively, I can trace my love of Nature to this seminal experience.

As Johnson indicates, this experience is by no means unique to me. As a Vision Quest guide, I have heard many similar stories from women and men seeking to go to the Sacred Mountains. For me, it is a testament to our indigenous roots in Nature—to our enduring, unbroken connection to Nature as our sacred home.

Johnson also makes the revealing point that, though moving and profound, this type of experience actually constitutes a wounding to the psyche of the young person. The experience thrusts a young person out of the unconscious innocence of childhood and into the painful awareness of another separate reality that, to his untutored mind, has little to do with everyday life. It is this awareness of duality, of a differentiation between the profane and the sacred, that plants a seed of longing in his heart.

Thus, the experience, though a blessing, also is experienced as a wound of separation. The unconscious wholeness of the garden of childhood is broken by the awareness of separation and duality. This experience of duality then becomes the cause of suffering and ultimately of the spiritual quest to reconcile the opposites. If all goes well in the process of individuation—the dynamic process by which we come to understand who we are and what we want to do with our lives—we will reunite the duality of inner and outer reality into a harmonious whole, except now with conscious awareness.

This psychological template of human development echoes more ancient mythological renderings of a three-staged unfolding of the human journey. For instance, we see it in the Biblical narrative of Adam and Eve's fall from innocence in the Garden of Eden.

The Garden represents humanity in an original unconscious unity with Creation. The Fall signals a rupture in this unconscious unity when Adam and Eve become consciousness of good and evil after tasting the forbidden fruit—Original Sin—and with it become aware of duality. A sinful humanity is then redeemed through atonement (at-one-ment) with God in a reconstituted Earth (Heaven on Earth).

Likewise, as the psychologist Erich Neumann points out in *The Origins and the History of Consciousness*, in creation myths from around the world, the primordial state is often depicted as an Uroboros, a circular image of a snake or dragon biting its own tail, or as a world egg that contains the World Parents (Heaven and Earth, the masculine and feminine opposites) lying "one on top of the other in the round, spacelessly and timelessly united, for as yet nothing has come between them to create duality out of the original unity." Then a rupture in this seamless unity occurs marking the birth of man and woman, and consciousness of the Other. The drama that then unfolds is depicted as the archetypal Hero's Journey to recover the original unity.

These mythological dramas can be viewed as a metaphorical rendering of the individuation process. From a psychological perspective, the primordial state is analogous to the unconscious, symbiotic union of infant and mother. This seamless unity is followed by the gradual emergence of an ego separate from mother, and with it the consciousness of duality. The birth of the ego then sets the stage for the drama of human development, as the individual seeks to consciously reunite with this original sense of oneness.

In other words, the cosmic drama is reenacted through the Heroic Journey of the individual toward the simultaneous realization of an inner wholeness and conscious oneness with the world. The inner experience of wholeness transforms the way the individual sees the world. The wholeness (holiness) of the Self and the oneness (holiness) of the world are two aspects of the same reality, inner and outer realities reflecting each other.

> Little Mouse could hardly believe his eyes. But there they were! But then he fell back to Earth, and he landed in the river! Little Mouse became frightened and scrambled back to the bank. He was wet and frightened nearly to death.
>
> "You have tricked me!" Little Mouse screamed at the Frog.
>
> "Wait," said Frog. "You are not harmed. Do not let your fear and anger blind you. What did you see?"
>
> "I," Little Mouse stammered, "I, I saw the Sacred Mountains!"
>
> "And you have a new name!" Frog said. "It is Jumping Mouse."

Little Mouse has taken a leap of faith only to fall back to Earth and then tumble into the river. After almost drowning in the river, he is frightened nearly to death. It is no joking matter to fall into the River of Life, to be immersed in the Waters of Life. Where will the river take him? What will be demanded of him? Will he drown in this powerful medicine? Moreover, this brush with death is really a foreshadowing of the symbolic death that lies ahead for Little Mouse if he is to reach the Sacred Mountains.

But Little Mouse feels betrayed by Frog and is angry. Frog gives him good counsel when he says, "Do not let your fear and anger blind you." Momentarily succumbing to fear and anger, Little Mouse has already forgotten his vision of the Sacred Mountains. We forget so easily. So quickly we let our fear and anger get in the way of perceiving reality clearly. Losing sight of the radiant mountains, we fall victim to the short-sighted concerns and fears of the ego. But Frog gently asks him, "What did you see?" He reminds him of his glimpse of the Sacred Mountains. He reminds him of what is really important, what he came here for, what his intention is. And he gives him a new name: Jumping Mouse.

Traditionally, among some American Indian tribes, when a young person returns from a quest, he tells the story of his quest in the Elder's Council. His story reveals aspects of his true nature, upon which his medicine name is based. His medicine name comes as a blessing to the heart of the young person for it signifies his true nature and marks his change in existential status from a child to a man. Of course, with this new name comes new responsibilities: he must live up to the name.

The Return

Upon his return from the Great River, Jumping Mouse suffers another wounding. His community does not welcome him as a hero returning from a great adventure. Instead, Jumping Mouse is spurned; indeed, he is regarded as "poison." This collective rejection represents the inertia of consensus reality resisting the introduction of a new way of perceiving reality. The influence of consensus reality can be so strong that it may also cause a part of Jumping Mouse to doubt his vision and to resist its challenging implications. The rejection and isolation that Jumping Mouse experiences initiates a descent into suffering. His suffering has many different layers.

At one layer, Jumping Mouse experiences loneliness, for he is without friends and is no longer supported by his community. He goes unrecognized for who he is and what he has seen. Indeed, at the deepest layer, it is precisely his vision of the Sacred Mountains that separates him from his fellow mice, for it represents the birth of a heightened consciousness that sets him apart from the other mice, who remain submerged in unconsciousness.

The suffering that Jumping Mouse experiences now is a wound of awareness. Before his journey to the river, he was unconscious of anything more to life than what lay right before his nose. Now he is aware of the Sacred Mountains, of the sacred dimension to life, and he cannot forget his vision of them. So now a longing to go to these mountains shadows his days among his people. Although his vision is a great blessing, the task of bringing it to fulfillment can be experienced as a great challenge, with much uncertainty and much risk. Business as usual, although he may try to escape into it, is really no longer an option for him; he has had a glimpse of another radiant reality, and he cannot turn his back on it.

Another aspect of Jumping Mouse's loneliness is that each of us is alone in our relationship to Spirit. Ultimately, each of us must find, or not find, our own path to Spirit. The search can be a lonely one, as it is for Jumping Mouse, especially in our times, when for many people the traditional religious institutions have lost their relevance. To find a way to the sacred in this age of materialism, cynicism, and outright nihilism is certainly a lonely pursuit, especially because it involves setting sail on uncharted seas. But the courage of Jumping Mouse can give us a strong heart as we face the unknown of our own journeys.

If Jumping Mouse allows himself to feel his loneliness at its deepest layer, he will touch and be touched by the loneliness that is a fundamental part of our human experience. This loneliness speaks of a suffering that is inseparable from living and that no one can take away.

In some respects, Jumping Mouse is drawing nearer to the First Noble Truth of the Buddha, which states, "All is suffering." No one, no creature, is exempt from suffering: all beings experience change and loss and are subject to sickness, aging, and death. So, this loneliness carries a foreshadowing of death, since each of us must face death alone: no one else can die for us.

Jumping Mouse's descent into the ashes of suffering is virtually inevitable after leaping so high and having a glimpse of Spirit. One cannot live permanently at such heights—the transcendent perspective will only perpetuate the division between the world and Spirit. Awareness demands that we return to the world and begin the process of integrating our vision in our everyday life. This return to the world will deepen Jumping Mouse's soul and bring his awareness to maturity.

When he returns to the world, Jumping Mouse's vision will sensitize him to the suffering of his fellow mice who live in ignorance of their true nature, and in response to their suffering his heart will open. Jumping Mouse will now exist between worlds, just as his guide Frog does. He knows the pain of living an unconscious life and has had a glimpse of the freedom of awakening. His new position as a threshold figure will teach him the Medicine Power that Frog offered him.

With this Medicine Power, Jumping Mouse will become a messenger between worlds and a healer. But before Jumping Mouse can fully embody this power he has a long journey ahead of him across the everyday world of the Prairie, where an even greater suffering and symbolic death will be demanded of him.

* * *

We have come to a break in our story. The story does not say how long Jumping Mouse lived among his people before setting out on the second stage of his journey to the Sacred Mountains. In the dreamlike realm of story it could have been many years. Jumping Mouse could have married, had children, gotten a job, and established himself in his world before the memory of the Sacred Mountains became a fire in his soul that compelled him to resume his search. As the renowned psychologist Carl Jung claimed, the individuation process doesn't take on full force, if at all, until midlife, after an individual has set down roots in the world.

But before we travel with Jumping Mouse across the Prairie, it might be helpful to pause and look back over the ground we have covered. In the next chapter, we will explore the archetypal dynamic of rites of passage in greater depth as a way to enrich our understanding of the first stage of Jumping Mouse's journey, and to emphasize the importance of such a rite for our modern world.

Rites of Passage:

An Archetypal Blueprint

*...there is a thinking in primordial images, in symbols which are
older than the historical man, which are inborn in him from the
earliest times, and, eternally living, outlasting generations, still
make up the groundwork of the human psyche. It is only possible
to live the fullest life when we are in harmony with these symbols;
wisdom is a return to them.*

— C. G. JUNG

In *The Hero with a Thousand Faces*, the mythologist Joseph Campbell discusses the structure of a "monomyth," a central motif underlying many myths and folk tales from around the world and across the centuries. The outward appearance of the monomyth assumes many different culturally and geographically determined trappings but represents an archetypal pattern that is a fundamental feature of "the groundwork of the human psyche." Symbolically, it reveals the innate human thrust toward self-awareness and transformation: the story of the Hero's Journey.

The Hero's Journey unfolds in three stages. In the first stage, "Departure," the individual hears the "Call to Adventure," much as Little Mouse hears the roaring in his ears and sets out on a journey of self-discovery and transformation. This motif, for instance, is found in the classic hero myth from our Western European tradition, *The Legend of the Holy Grail.*

The story begins with a boy who interestingly does not seem to have a name. Like Little Mouse, he does not yet have a clear sense of who he is. While in the forest one day, he sees five knights in resplendent garb ride by and is filled with a passion to follow them and become a knight.

The knights in shining armor are akin to the Sacred Mountains that Little Mouse sees: each represents those unforgettable experiences when the heart first opens in wonder. Inspired by his vision, the boy leaves his weeping mother behind and ventures forth on a great adventure.

In the second stage, "Initiation," the individual wanders through the dark forest of the unknown, symbolic of the unknown dimensions of his own being. Here he encounters all sorts of adversaries and dragons that seek to defeat him, but through the aid of allies that represent his own previously unknown inner resources, the individual defeats the inner dragons of self-doubt, fear, and ignorance.

In the Grail legend, the boy discovers that his name is Parsifal, which means Innocent Fool. His name signifies that he must humble himself and become like a child again, innocent and trusting, if he is to realize the fullness of his humanity. Little Mouse follows a similar path of letting go of his self-centeredness and surrendering to the whisperings of Spirit in order to discover his true nature.

In the third and final stage, "Return," the hero returns triumphant to his community with the boon of self-knowledge. In turn, the wisdom of self-knowledge—the awakening of human consciousness to a new level of awareness—serves as a gift to the community through which it is regenerated from the state of decline that it had fallen into prior to his departure. The returning hero models a new way of being in the world that galvanizes the hearts and minds of his community.

The anthropologist Arnold Van Gennep discovered a threefold structure similar to that of the hero myth in the initiation ceremonies of indigenous peoples from around the world. He referred to these three stages as severance, initiation, and incorporation.

Among indigenous peoples, the passage from childhood to adulthood was regarded as momentous; indeed, it was seen as a second birth. The first birth was into the family and tribal matrix in which a child was sheltered and nurtured in his innocence, trust, and unconsciousness. Within this protected cocoon, a child gradually developed a deep sense of belonging to the natural world, of being bodily rooted and at home in the world. The second birth was out of the family matrix into a wider, more expansive matrix, which was based on realizing a sacred relationship to the Earth and to all her life forms as manifestations of Spirit. This new spiritual ground then became the foundation for adulthood and for the emergence into self-awareness.

Elaborate rites of passage were created to foster a successful transition from childhood to adulthood. These rites began with the separation of the child from the family, from all that was familiar and known, habitual and routine, maternal and safe. In one African tribe, for instance, the elders would come in the middle of the night to abduct the child and take him to the initiatory ground far removed from village life.

The mothers of the children would wail and pull out their hair at the loss of their child. In part they were being melodramatic, for this drama had been enacted since the time of the ancestors, so they knew that it was coming and that it was necessary. But at the same time, they knew that when their child returned to the village after the initiation rites they would no longer be a child and would no longer live with them in their hut.

Although some initiatory rites involved bloodletting and other practices that are repellent to our Western sensibilities, we need not let these practices blind us to the primary intention of rites of passage: to create the conditions for the possibility of a direct, unmediated experience of Spirit. To achieve this end the elders revealed the deeper spiritual significance of the myths and stories the children had been hearing since a young age, such as the story of Jumping Mouse. They also had the initiates undergo various ordeals that were designed to break through their habitual ways of perceiving reality, so that they would be open to an experience of Spirit.

For example, in the *Healing Wisdom of Africa,* Malidoma Somé, an African man who left his tribe to be educated in the West and then later returned to his tribal village to be initiated, relates a powerful story about an initiatory rite that he underwent.

He and the other initiates were placed before different trees in the jungle and instructed to remain there until the spirit of their tree spoke to them. After all the other initiates had returned, Malidoma remained before his tree. Fearing that his Westernized, rational mind would block him from ever hearing the spirit of the tree, he returned to the elders with a fabricated story. Their response was to laugh at his concoction and to send him back out to his tree.

After a few days of sitting before the tree, he finally experienced the spirit of the tree. The tree was transformed into a woman. He thought of her as the "green lady" because her skin was green, but really, as he describes her, "she was green from the inside out, as if her body were filled with green fluid … this green was the expression of immeasurable love." Not knowing how he got there, he found himself in her loving embrace. He describes this experience as "a homecoming of the utmost healing."

This experience, so alien to our rational minds, changed Malidoma's life forever. He describes the change it brought about in him:

> Nature shows itself in some unique way to every individual during his or her initiation, and I know of the stories of many other people who have been touched in this way by nature. The deepest dimension of my own transformation came about through being touched in this way. My jumpy doubting began to find some rest. The fires of alienation, pride, and anger began to be quenched by the waters of accepting love. I no longer felt like a proud, wounded outsider.

The experience with the green lady resolved that, for all of a sudden I belonged… She changed me from deep inside. She allowed me to break through the wall of perception that my Western education had erected in me, and she connected me intimately with nature, the way my fellow villagers experienced it. She brought me back home.

Based on this initiatory experience, Malidoma became an eloquent spokesperson for the wisdom of the indigenous way of life and the healing capacity of ritual and Nature.

In *Rites and Symbols of Initiation*, the scholar of comparative religion Mircea Eliade makes the point that, among indigenous peoples, a symbolic initiatory death is seen as necessary for the commencement of a spiritual life, which in turn is regarded as a condition for entering adulthood. The life-altering significance of the transition from childhood to adulthood demands an equally powerful ritual to mark it: a symbolic ritual of death and rebirth. The child must symbolically die in order for the adult to be born. Childhood innocence and irresponsibility must die in order for the individual to assume adult responsibilities.

The wisdom of the indigenous mind is the awareness of the necessity of this symbolic death. Included in this is the awareness that in order for an individual to leave behind the comfort and security of the maternal matrix, he must establish a new matrix in the arms of Spirit by means of an unmediated experience of that reality. Such an initiatory experience satisfies an archetypal blueprint that has been hard-wired in our psyches since time immemorial and demands to be met.

The individual's relationship to Spirit as revealed in Nature then becomes the new ground for his standing in the world and the source of his power in the world. And this power is not a power *over* the things of the world as power in the West is conceived; rather, it is a power *with and through* Nature. In other words, it is not a nonrelational, conquering power but rather a relational power that flows from an intimate connection and partnership with the beings of the world.

After undergoing the ordeals of initiation, the initiates return to the tribe and are welcomed back with celebrations, clearly marking and honoring their change in existential status from a boy to a man, or from a girl to a woman. Now, of course, they are faced with the new and in many ways more difficult challenge of incorporating their initiatory experience into their life as an adult. This return and its attendant challenges mark the entrance into the stage of Incorporation.

In The Story of Jumping Mouse, we can clearly see these three initiatory stages. Hearing the roaring in his ears, Little Mouse is called to separate from the safe, known world of the mice and to journey through unknown territory to the Great River. His initiatory experience is his glimpse of the Sacred Mountains off in the distance. His experience of the sacred dimension that permeates the natural world thrusts him out of his unconscious absorption in Nature and identification with the collective. In short, he awakens to the immanent reality of Spirit that transcends the subject-object duality of ordinary consciousness, and at the same he begins to individuate from the collective.

As acknowledgment of Little Mouse's leap of faith and show of courage, he is given a new name. His renaming marks the importance of his transformation from an unconscious collective persona to a unique individuated person, from a conditioned mouse to a perceiving mouse, from unconsciousness to awareness.

But upon his return to his people, instead of being acknowledged for his accomplishment, Jumping Mouse is rejected. He now lives among the other mice as an outsider, but the memory of the Sacred Mountains burns in his mind and heart. In this regard, the archetypal dynamic of rites of passage has *not* been carried through to its completion. For one thing, there has been no formal incorporation phase, during which Jumping Mouse would be welcomed back by his community and given opportunities for the fruit of his experience to grow and ripen.

In a traditional indigenous society, Jumping Mouse's vision of the Sacred Mountains would be affirmed and cultivated. He would be taught by the tribal elders the deeper meaning of his vision and shown ways to build upon it, in order to foster its full blossoming within his heart. Thus, Jumping Mouse's rite of passage was not completed because his vision was not affirmed by the collective; the circle had not been made complete. Furthermore, he only had a glimpse of the Sacred Mountains. His experience can be likened to a premature opening to the sacred that was spoken of in the previous chapter. This existential situation of an uncompleted archetypal dynamic that begs for completion sets up the conditions for his journey to the Sacred Mountains in the second part of the story.

When we look at our society today, we see that this existential situation of an uncompleted or, as is more often the case, a completely interrupted archetypal dynamic, accurately describes the situation that our youth find themselves in. As Steven Foster says in the documentary, *Lost Borders: Coming of Age in the Wilderness*, adolescents in our society are like a plane revving up on a runway but with nowhere to go.

At an unconscious, archetypal level, all the tremendous energies of adolescents are building toward an experience that can clearly mark their successful transition to adulthood. There is a powerful, innate urge in them to complete this archetypal blueprint. However, in our culture, instead of being provided a safe container within which these archetypal energies may be skillfully and lovingly nurtured and channeled, all they find is a gaping void. They are suffering in this void.

The Adolescent Passage Today

The archetypal dynamic that finds expression in formal initiation rites among indigenous people—severance, initiation, and incorporation—captures the inner psychological landscape that adolescents from any time or place find themselves dealing with already. In other words, the outer ceremony simply gives formal acknowledgment of an inner dynamic that needs to be brought to a heightened awareness and completion, not only for the sake of the individual but also for the continued vitality of the community.

All of the psycho-spiritual elements intrinsic to a process of inner transformation at any stage in life are thrown into bold relief within the dynamic of the adolescent rite of passage. As the prototypical rite of passage experience, it warrants closer examination.

Adolescents are often engaged in an inner quest for identity, which can be quite passionate and at the same time quite anguishing. They are asking themselves the big questions: Who am I? Where did I come from? Where am I going? Ideally, they have grown and developed within the family cocoon, nurtured by its care and supported by its beliefs and values. Now it is time for them to find their own wings, to take flight out of the family nest, and to discover their own beliefs and values, which may be very different from those of their families and, in some cases, from those of their culture.

For many young people, this second passage through the birth canal can be very painful, fraught with anxiety, depression, fear, longing, hopelessness, and despair. For those who seamlessly adopt the beliefs and values of their families and the mainstream culture the passage can be smooth, but then later on in life they may be forced by either inner or outer circumstances to reassess what is important to them. When they enter the proverbial midlife transition, it may be more painful for them because of their earlier passing over of these central existential questions that beg to be addressed in a way that is based on their own direct experience.

Yet even as adolescents give shape to their own unique identity and psychologically separate from the family matrix, they are simultaneously driven by a strong desire to belong to a larger social context that can serve as a source of meaning and purpose. This need to belong can find expression in many outlets—from sports to work, to social, religious, and political associations. Often it finds expression in a fiery idealism that is fed by a desire to make the world a better place. In today's world many young people are at a loss, however, to find a larger context of meaning into which they can channel their inner fire.

In the pre-industrial world there were family farms, vocational guilds offering apprenticeships, and strong religious institutions that provided stable structures and a context of meaning for young people in transition to the adult world. Within these vocational and religious structures, a young person could experience a strong sense of belonging and of contributing to society. As such, these opportunities and structures provided young people with meaningful avenues for self-expression, self-identity, and self-esteem.

In postmodern times, for many young people, the traditional religious institutions, due to irrelevancy and ossification, have lost their appeal. There are few opportunities for apprenticeships. The industrial workplace has become increasing destabilized as corporations downsize and seek the cheapest labor markets overseas. And the corporate workplace is riddled with greed, backbiting ambition, criminal malfeasance, and a bottom-line mentality that places profit over people and the environment. Such a world does not adequately meet the idealism of youth, and as a consequence many young people feel useless, adrift, and hopeless.

So adolescents find themselves standing on the threshold of the adult world trying to figure out where they might fit in and how they might be able to make things better. Their threshold position, unburdened (at least for a while) by either a clearly defined social role or economic necessity, gives them a vantage point from which they can see more clearly into the state of our world. From their threshold position, they can feel more acutely the suffering our society is undergoing at this critical juncture in history. Unwittingly, like canaries in the coal mines, they become a touchstone by which we may measure the health of our society.

According to the National Institute of Mental Health, each year in the United States 250,000 adolescents attempt suicide, and 2,000 succeed in taking their own lives. Since 1960, the adolescent suicide rate has doubled. These figures do not include deaths in car accidents and other risk-taking deaths, which in some cases may be acts of suicide. In addition, 8.3 percent of adolescents in the United States suffer from depression. But these statistics only indicate what is reported. If we factor in all the cases that go unreported, which no doubt far exceed those reported, depression may be a quiet epidemic.

Based on these statistics, which indicate an alarming increase in depression and suicide among our young people, the health of our society is not good, to say the least. Then there's the pervasive alcohol and substance abuse among the young, as they seek to self-medicate their pain and/or get a taste of Spirit that they so long for. The rise in the seemingly unprovoked violence of adolescents is also a very disturbing indicator that all is not well in our land of affluence. Something is amiss in America, and our increasing reliance upon diagnoses and pharmaceutical remedies does not address their pain; rather, it sends them deeper into despair.

Our young people are crying out in pain, roaring in our ears. It seems that few are listening. By and large, this momentous passage into adulthood goes virtually unrecognized. The religious coming-of-age ceremonies such as Christian confirmation and Jewish bar/bat mitzvah are more or less perfunctory among the mainstream population; they do not come close to equaling the power and mystery of the ancient rites of passage among indigenous people. The other more typical and pedestrian societal markers of entrance to adulthood, such as graduating from high school, getting one's driver's license, being able to drink legally, vote, or join the military, and going off to college, do not adequately address the archetypal need for a powerful initiatory experience.

In the absence of any formal recognition of the significance of this passage, adolescents are pretty much left to themselves to create their own rites of passage. Regrettably, these peer initiations are often dangerous and self-destructive, involving high risk-taking, alcohol and drug abuse, violence, premature sexuality, teen pregnancies, and in the worse case scenarios, suicide and death.

Instinctively, adolescents know that they need to be initiated: they know that they need to have their mettle tested in order to feel inside that they are no longer a dependent child and are worthy of independent adult status. That is why they engage in risk-taking and brush up as close to death as they can and still talk about it. They are drawn to extremes that place them on the edge of life and death, because they also know instinctively that that is where transformation takes place. At an unconscious level, they also know that they need to have their armored hearts broken open in order for the beauty and passion that burns inside them to burst forth into the world. Their inexpressible longing roars in their ears that they need to be touched by the fire of Spirit.

The failure of our culture to understand and respond to the archetypal dynamic of the quest creates the conditions under which young people act out in self-destructive and high risk-taking behaviors. Unfortunately, we tend to pathologize these behaviors, which admittedly can be dangerous and unhealthy, rather than address the underlying need that is not being met. In doing so, we tend to pathologize the very nature of the quest itself, rather than seeing its inherent necessity and beauty. As a result, young people who are in the midst of a tremendous inner search for meaning tend to see themselves in a negative way, through the critical eyes of the culture. They feel like there is something intrinsically wrong with them. A consequence of the culture's rejection is that they are driven deeper into despair and desperation.

As Jung indicates in the epigraph to this chapter, wisdom would be a return to the collective recognition of the archetypal necessity of rites of passage, adapted to meet the needs, fears, and longings of today's youth. As a culture, it is imperative that we find ways to respond to the cries of our youth, for as the mythologist Michael Meade warns in *Men and the Water of Life:*

> In tribal cultures, it was said that if the boys were not initiated into manhood, if they were not shaped by the skills and love of the elders, then they would destroy the culture. If the fires that innately burn inside youths are not intentionally and lovingly added to the hearth of the community, they will burn down the structures of culture, just to feel the warmth.

In our culture, the unmet fires of our youth are, by and large, not being turned outward upon the structures of culture, but rather are being turned inward in self-loathing and self-destructive acts. All the same, the price is obviously too great to pay.

In the next chapter, we will take a closer look at some of today's youth in transition and at the beauty of the quest experience through a Vision Quest program that I led for a small group of incoming college students.

3

Stories from the Threshold:

A Wilderness Rite of Passage
for Adolescents

The Vision Quest described here followed the three-stage structure discussed in the previous chapter—severance, initiation, and incorporation.

The severance phase began when these young people left behind their family, friends, and everyday lives and continued during the four days prior to their departure for their solitary Vision Quest. During this phase the participants were being prepared mentally, emotionally, physically, and spiritually to face the challenge of spending three days and nights alone fasting in Nature. This is no small feat, considering our Western disconnection from Nature.

An important feature of preparation involves activities that are designed to help participants open up to the intuitive dimension of their being, instead of relying exclusively upon their rational minds, as we are conditioned to do in Western culture.

Another way to view these activities would be to see them as attempts to help participants gain access to the indigenous soul that lies buried within them beneath the veneer of civilization. After all, compared to the tens of thousands of years that humans lived an indigenous way of life in an intimate, interdependent connection with Nature, the span of civilization, especially if we just consider the mere 250 years of our mechanized, industrialized world, is relatively small. Although certainly atrophied and resisted, this indigenous soul can be accessed through the power of silence, solitude, and fasting in Nature.

Many of the preparation exercises are designed to break through the control mechanisms that we habitually and automatically use to protect ourselves. These control mechanisms prevent us from accessing the full vibrancy of the world around us. Some of these exercises are silent walking, blindfolded trust walks, night walking, meditation in Nature, shamanic journeying, and interspecies communication. Although some of these activities are difficult for Westerners to understand and engage in, they can often be quite powerful and revealing once one's resistance to them is overcome.

Another central feature of preparation is that participants are assisted in clarifying their intentions for undertaking a Vision Quest. Clarity with regard to one's intention is important because when things get difficult on their solos—when boredom, loneliness, fear, depression, or self-doubt arises (and something of this nature inevitably will come up)—a strong intention will help them stay the course.

In this context, setting an intention is different from setting a goal. Although goals certainly serve a purpose in our lives, intentions differ in that they are not attached to a particular outcome. Setting an intention is more akin to sounding your heart for what really matters to you, and then aligning your whole being with that. An intention is like a rudder on a boat: it helps you stay on course through rough waters.

Intentions are clarified within the context of participants telling their life stories in a group counsel process. Telling one's story, often for the first time, within the context of sacred ritual space, can be a profound experience. To be listened to from the heart, without judgment, without criticism, without analysis, gives people the safety to reveal and explore their lives as deeply as they wish to go. These are powerful moments, because the honesty, sincerity, and wisdom of young people are very touching.

Preparation also involves storytelling. Vision Quest leaders tell myths and folk tales with rites-of-passage motifs. For example, I tell The Story of Jumping Mouse the night before the participants cross the threshold into the sacred space of the Vision Quest.

These stories serve as symbolic stepping stones for the participants to enter into the richness of their own lives. They show them that they are not the only ones who have struggled with parents, inner demons, and the meaning of life. Through the stories, they are able to reimagine their lives and place their struggles and fears within a wider archetypal context of meaning.

The day before their quests, participants are sent out to find a solo site. When they return to base camp, we gather around the campfire. The participants talk about the process of finding a site and are asked to state their intention. That's where we enter their stories.

***

Linda—nicknamed Bionic Woman by the other participants because of her vitality and strength—seems desperate to win our acceptance. She engages with the others in a playful way, yet there is a marked social awkwardness to her. Linda tells us that when she was an infant her mother abandoned her. She says she has been dealing with depression her whole life. She tells us she's looking for somewhere in the world where she can feel "at home."

When Linda went out to find a Vision Quest site, her search was an ordeal. She selected four different sites but ended up rejecting each one for one reason or another. Finally, she found herself in some mud flats and decided to make it her home. The wisdom she drew from her ordeal was, "I need to make home wherever I am." She states that her intention in undertaking a Vision Quest is to learn to be giving. She finishes her story by telling us about a suicide attempt she made in the spring. The suicide attempt is news to me; she hadn't mentioned it in the medical history form participants fill out. I'm shaken by it, but further questioning reveals that she's not at risk.

I tell her that it took courage to inform us of her suicide attempt. I respond empathically to the wound of abandonment she suffered as a child and affirm the spiritual nature of her search for a "home." I also affirm her choice of the mud flats as a site, her willingness to look at the dark parts of herself and of her life. I tell her she has a wonderful exuberance and playfulness about her. I also tell her that her intention to give is a beautiful one, but she must be careful not to give at the expense of her own authenticity. Like other young people, indeed many of us no matter what age, Linda faces the developmental task of placing her own authenticity before her need for social approval, and not vice versa.

Kevin is quiet; he stands off a bit from the others. There's a stiffness to him, something weighing on him. He mentions trouble with his parents, which caused him to leave home and live on his own for a while. He found a site near Linda's. He chose a place where two beavers were playing in the lake. He was drawn by their playfulness. I reflect back to him that the beavers may represent a part of himself that is seeking to come out. He says that he used to be loud and rowdy, but it was all show. Now he wants to be honest and truthful. Like many young people, Kevin moves between extremes, trying on different personas as he seeks the truth of his own soul. His intention is to be open.

Bill, a natural storyteller, has an interest in world religions, especially Buddhism. He's amiable but a bit aloof. He has connected with Kevin. His parents are divorced; he lives with his dad. Bill chose a site on a spit of land sticking out into the western fork of the lake. A dream guided him to this place. He intends to remain in his purpose circle—a circle of stones representing one's true self—the whole length of his solo. He seeks awareness.

Paul, a gentle, easygoing, funny young man, says he's dealing with separating from an overprotective mother. His intention is to seek clarity and focus in his life, and to discover how to separate from his mother without using anger and rebellion. Paul found a sun-filled glade on an island as his site, a place that beautifully captures his spirit.

Maria is a fiery, compact ball of energy, enthusiasm, and goodwill. This is her first time camping and she's eager to learn new things. She says she has had a blessed life. Maria also encountered difficulty finding a site, which annoyed her because, as she said, "Things always work out for me." Almost at the point of giving up she came upon a large rock with a birch tree overhanging it. She decided it was time for her to lay down on her "Promethean rock" and learn about suffering. She intended to stay on her rock the whole time. Maria is a brave warrior, who faces her fears head-on, like her fear of the night.

Emma, at 17, is the youngest. She's always smoking and talking. She has multiple piercings. She looks like she would be more at home in a coffeehouse in Greenwich Village, but she's doing fine. Her parents are divorced. Her mother seemed more anxious than Emma when she dropped her off. Emma chose a site on the same island as Paul. She found a dead tree at the edge of the woods and the shore of the lake— symbolically the meeting place between worlds, between ordinary and nonordinary reality, between consciousness and the unconscious. The tree formed a natural seat, in which she lay down and immediately fell asleep. She says she felt held by the Goddess. Emma's intention is to discover who she is.

Carol is dealing with a painful past of sexual abuse. She plans on getting married in the near future. She found a beautiful site near a sandy beach on a small cove. She told herself it would be her site if she found a heart-shaped rock, representing her nickname, Big Heart. She found one. Her intention is to let go of her painful past.

* * *

With the completion of the preparation phase, the young people are ready to enter the initiation or threshold phase. A threshold is both a point of departure and a point of entrance. It places participants at the edge of their known world, filling them with both fear and excitement, like Little Mouse as he stood at the edge of the vast Prairie. Mythologically, it is a "betwixt and between" place, straddling life and death. At the border of the unknown, they are being called to die to the old and leap into the unknown of what is seeking to be born in them. It is a place charged with danger and adventure, of heightened awareness and mystery. As such, this threshold phase aptly reflects where adolescents find themselves in their lives. Like animals moving at the border of forest and meadow, they move in and out of immaturity and maturity, in and out of the shadows and the light, in and out of fear and longing, in and out of despair and hope.

The beauty of the Vision Quest is that the threshold where young people find themselves is ritually enacted as they depart into the unknown on their solitary journeys into the wilderness. The ritual heightens their awareness of the threshold and of the significance of the passage itself.

Alone, they enter the wilderness of Nature and the wilderness of themselves. In solitude and silence, they are given the opportunity to look deeply into themselves and reflect upon who and what they are. This is something they are doing anyway. The difference, however, is that this ritual provides an experience that heightens the possibility of insight, awareness, vision, and a heart opening to the Spirit in all things.

While in the threshold space, with their senses and minds sharpened by solitude, silence, and fasting, Nature acts as both the sacred ground and mirror of their souls. In Nature they see reflected the wild, free, and holy parts of themselves. As they sit alone in the depths of a forest, on the shores of a lake, or on a desert mesa, they can experience an opening to the life that moves within them and all around them; they can feel the interconnectedness of all the different life forms; they can sense the sacredness of all life.

In this opening, Nature begins to speak to them. Trees, rocks, deer, hawk, river, rain, wind—each speak of a soulful interiority, shine with a radiant luminosity, and reflect a way of being in the world that is accessible to anyone who can listen deeply.

As they sit alone, quiet and attentive, they can touch and be touched by the simple beauty and joy of being fully present to themselves and the world around them— maybe for the first time in their lives. This experience of being fully present in the moment is itself vision. With this vision they return to the core of their being, which is inseparable from the heart of the world.

* * *

The morning after their third night on the solo the questers return to base camp. This is always a special moment for me. One by one they trickle into camp, their faces shining with an inner peace. They are who they are. I greet each one with a prayer of gratitude for his or her safe return. They have undergone an ordeal, confronted their fears, and come through to the other side. A child could not spend three days and nights alone in the wilderness.

In the evening we gather around the fire in the growing darkness. A full moon sits on the rim of an eastern hill. Moonlight dances on the water and illumines the land and our faces with its silver light. The scene seems primal: a band of men and women gathered around a fire on the shore of a lake beneath a full moon, living close to Nature, close to our own nature, and close to each other. In a moment the stories of their Vision Quest experiences will begin. The air is charged with anticipation.

Hearing and responding to the stories is always a magical experience for me. I am lifted to another plane of being. As I respond to the stories, mirroring back to them the way their experiences in Nature reflect their own souls and gifts, as native peoples have practiced for thousands of years, the words and images that flow from me often surprise me. Truly a force greater than myself is moving through me to these young people, giving them the recognition—the elder's blessing—they so hunger for and so deserve.

And in this moment, the circle of giving is made complete, as I am in turn touched by the utter honesty and sweetness of their words. It is this circle of mutual reciprocity and respect, so lacking in the modern world, that holds together the things of the world and reenacts again and again the sacred interconnectedness of life.

Linda struggled with depression and thoughts of suicide. But she built a Medicine Wheel, which had been discussed in the preparation phase, and prayed to the four directions. This strengthened her. Then while out walking she came across a wild blueberry bush overflowing with berries. She felt a strong desire to give to the other questers, so she gathered the berries and thought of each person questing with her. With this selfless act of communion, her depression lifted. Later she stripped naked, covered her body with mud, and dived into the lake, washing herself clean of her dark thoughts. She emerged from her self-created baptismal cleansed and feeling fully alive.

Kevin drew a bird on a large stone and christened it "Flynn's Firebird," based on a Russian folktale that I had told earlier. I tell him it isn't my firebird but his—the firebird of passion that lies locked up in his soul, waiting to take flight in the words that shape his poems. I honor his inwardness, his silence, and his struggle to be open and honest. Kevin spent a lot of time meditating on the beavers that lived, worked, and played near his site. He longs for the freedom, balance, and spontaneity of his true nature.

As intended, Bill did not leave his purpose circle. He sat resolute under his tarp tipi at the edge of the lake, gazing out across the waters of his soul, like the Buddha. Bill seems like an old soul. His sparkling blue eyes evoke images of windswept, snow-streaked mountain places high in Tibet or Nepal. He is an ancient monk who has reincarnated in the modern world in order to restore the memory of the peace and stillness of the sage to our noisy, busy lives. He recites one of his poems, leaving us spellbound. The poem describes himself as a reluctant messenger who prefers silence to words, solitude to company, Nature to civilization. I marvel at the breadth and depth of understanding of this 18-year-old.

Paul was restless and struggled with thoughts of returning. He reasoned that it was stupid to be out on his island alone without food. The ascetic path was not the way of Spirit. Hadn't the Buddha discovered that, when he chose the middle path between asceticism and indulgence? If all he could think about was food, how was he going to be open to Spirit? At one point he picked up a stick and started beating it repeatedly against his cup. After a while he began to sing along with the rhythm. Sound and song carried him to the interior of his wild heart. On his own he had discovered an ancient technique for inducing an altered state of consciousness—drumming and chanting. Through this experience he gained greater clarity about who he was, and this clarity helped him to separate from his mother with love.

Maria faced her loneliness as she sat on her rock. Gradually, she discriminated between her natural tendency to get lonely and her capacity to be alone. As she watched a solitary loon diving deep into the lake, she realized that she was not alone: all of Nature was with her. As she delved into her aloneness, a deeper appreciation of all aspects of her life grew inside her, especially her relationships with loved ones. Listening to Maria was like witnessing a flower as it unfolds into the fullness of its splendor.

Once again Emma curled up into the hollow of her dead tree and slept. She slept most of the time she was out on her solo. She said she didn't want to look inside because she was afraid she would find nothing there. My heart went out to her. I wanted to take her into my arms and tell her everything would be all right. But, even as she slept, the Great Mother was holding her in her arms. Perhaps it was too soon for Emma to leave the womb of protection and innocence. She was like the lizard tatooed at the base of her spine: her energies lay curled up in repose deep within her, both awaiting and in fear of the transformation into adulthood beckoning to her from the other side.

Carol wrestled with demons of betrayal and a flickering self-worth. She stripped off her clothes and swam in the lake, wishing to wash herself clean of her tainted past. She swam furiously, the fury inside her erupting. She emerged from the waters and set her mind on her upcoming marriage. But her dreams told her that her demons would not be put to rest so easily. She was being called into a heroic struggle with a wound that haunts her. But she carries her heart-shaped rock as a reminder of the purity of her heart and her capacity to love and be loved. She is Big Heart, and no one can take that away from her.

***

After hearing the stories we hold a Sweat Lodge Ceremony, an ancient American Indian ritual of death and rebirth, symbolically marking the transformation each quester has undergone. In the heat of the lodge we pray, sing, laugh, tell stories, and howl like a pack of wolves. Linda sums up the feelings of all of us when she says, "I can't stop smiling, I'm so happy."

* * *

In indigenous societies, after completing a rite of passage such as this, the young person is embraced by the tribe as a man or woman. They have surrendered dependence for independence, irresponsibility for responsibility. They have left the family matrix with the promise of belonging to the larger whole as an adult. In failing to offer meaningful rites of passage, our society does not extend that promise to its young people, thereby making separation from the family matrix all that much harder.

The modern adaptation of the Vision Quest attempts to fill this societal void. It can never equal the power of these ancient rites, because it does not have the full support of the community, but it does serve the important function of assisting young people in developing the qualities of soul necessary for becoming the unique person each of them is.

The very nature of silence, solitude, and fasting forces individuals to face themselves and their fears, and in so doing deepens their capacity for self-reflection, self-awareness, and self-possession. Moreover, it gives them the unique opportunity to taste the peace and joy that comes with being at one with oneself and Nature and Spirit. These are all qualities of soul that will serve them well on their journeys into manhood and womanhood, indeed on their path toward wholeness.

PART TWO

Initiation:

Journey to the Sacred Mountains

Perhaps the most important reason for lamenting [a Vision Quest] is that it helps us to realize our oneness with all things, to know all things are our relatives; and then in behalf of all things we pray to Wakan Tanka that He may give us knowledge of Him who is the source of all things, yet greater than all things.

—*BLACK ELK, OGLALA LAKOTA MEDICINE MAN*

The Old Mouse:

A Failure of Imagination

Destructiveness is the outcome of unlived life. Those individuals and social conditions that make for suppression of life produce the passion for destruction.

—ERICH FROMM

Jumping Mouse lived again among his People, but he could not forget his vision of the Sacred Mountains. The memory burned in the mind and heart of Jumping Mouse, and one day he went to the edge of the River Place…

Jumping Mouse went to the edge of the Place of Mice and looked out onto the Prairie. He looked up for eagles. The sky was full of many spots, each one an eagle. But he was determined to go to the Sacred Mountains. He gathered all of his courage and ran just as fast as he could onto the Prairie. His little heart pounded with excitement and fear.

He ran until he came to a stand of sage. He was resting and trying to catch his breath when he saw an old mouse. The patch of sage Old Mouse lived in was a haven for mice. Seeds were plentiful, and there was nesting material and many things to be busy with.

"Hello," said Old Mouse. "Welcome."

Jumping Mouse was amazed. Such a place and such a mouse! "You are truly a great mouse," Jumping Mouse said, with all the respect he could find. "This is truly a wonderful place. And the eagles cannot see you here, either," Jumping Mouse said.

"Yes," said Old Mouse, "and one can see all the beings of the Prairie here: Buffalo, Antelope, Rabbit, and Coyote. One can see them all from here and know their names."

"That is marvelous," Jumping Mouse said. "Can you also see the river and the Great Mountains?"

"Yes and no," Old Mouse said with conviction. "I know there is the Great River. But I am afraid that the Great Mountains are only a myth. Forget your passion to see them and stay here with me. There is everything you want here, and it is a good place to be."

"How can he say such a thing?" thought Jumping Mouse. "The Medicine of the Sacred Mountains is nothing one can forget."

"Thank you very much for the meal you have shared with me, Old Mouse, and also for sharing your great home," Jumping Mouse said. "But I must seek the Mountains."

"You are a foolish mouse to leave here. There is danger on the Prairie! Look up there!" Old Mouse said, with even more conviction. "See all those spots! They are eagles, and they will catch you!"

Once you've had a glimpse of the possibilities that lie waiting to flower within you, it is impossible to forget and go back to busying yourself with the details of daily living as though the Sacred Mountains did not exist. However, the task that your vision places on you can be so intimidating that at times you may resist it. Or, the pervasive consensus reality of our consumption-oriented culture may temporarily lull you, like a child's lullaby, into sleepwalking and forgetfulness. As we get caught up in the details of daily life, each of us can slip in and out of wakefulness and forgetfulness, just like Wolf in our story.

Nonetheless, each of us also has moments of wakefulness when we remember that, as the French existentialist philosopher Albert Camus put it, "A man's work is nothing more than to rediscover, through the detours of art, those one or two images in the presence of which his heart first opened."

Here we may conceive of art in the broadest possible way as the work through which a person's heart and soul finds revelation and expression in the world. Such work springs from the well of creative imagination from which the poetic, artistic, and mythic consciousness within each of us draws. And, indeed, it is the opening of Jumping Mouse's heart before the vision of the Sacred Mountains that one day brings him to the edge of the "River Place" again.

The Prairie stretches out, vast and unknown, in front of Jumping Mouse. It is new and exciting, but also intimidating. High up in the blue sky, eagles wheel effortlessly on thermals and pierce the ground with their steely gaze as they seek out a tender morsel like Jumping Mouse. The Austrian poet Rainer Maria Rilke captures this moment of decision well in his beautiful *Book of Hours*:

Summer was like your house: you knew where each thing stood
Now you must go out into your heart as onto a vast plain
Now the immense loneliness begins.

Jumping Mouse has moved to the edge of his known world and stands before the unknown of his yet-to-be-lived life. On the threshold of the possible, he finds the courage and takes off across the Prairie; his heart beats with excitement and fear. The unknown world awaits him with all of its beauty and chaos, its comforts and challenges, its allies and adversaries, its joys and sorrows, its lessons and temptations, just as it awaits each of us in each moment of our lives.

Jumping Mouse's first encounter on his journey across the Prairie is Old Mouse, who lives in a "Haven for Mice." Jumping Mouse is truly impressed with Old Mouse and the wonderful place he lives in. Not only is there everything a mouse could ever need but also Old Mouse is hidden from the eagles overhead. Old Mouse has set himself up pretty nicely: his life is one of ease and comfort, free from danger. Yet his way of being is narrowly circumscribed by the material plane of existence.

It makes sense that Jumping Mouse's first encounter on the way to the Sacred Mountains would be someone who represents the temptations of a worldly existence, devoid of a spiritual dimension. A life of material satisfaction and security could easily appear very attractive, as opposed to a spiritual journey filled with risk and uncertainty regarding its outcome. But Jumping Mouse does not fall for the temptation, and his opinion of Old Mouse plummets when Old Mouse informs him that he knows of the Great River but that the Great Mountains are only a myth.

Old Mouse is an exemplar of consensus reality. He champions an egoic attachment to material reality and untempered greed. Concerned only with feathering his own nest, his life revolves around protecting his own self-interests and bolstering his own self-importance. In his world, he is Numero Uno—the acme of hubris. In his self-satisfied arrogance, he is unable to see beyond the tip of his nose to the Sacred Mountains off in the distance.

Although this depiction of Old Mouse may seem extreme, each of us can probably recognize aspects of him in ourselves. He represents our instinctive inclination to keep ourselves safe, sheltered, and well fed. He represents that gut feeling we have of being a separate self, concerned primarily with securing our own safety and comfort, with trying to get our own way and being in control, and with ceaselessly competing with others for finite goodies.

The self-centered, materialist orientation to life that Old Mouse exemplifies is the dominant paradigm of our culture. It finds validation and exaltation in our ideal of the rugged, autonomous individual, who battles against all odds and adversaries to achieve monetary success and power.

From an early age, we are encouraged (especially males) to be competitive and aggressive on the battlefield of life and to divide the world into shifting camps of friends and enemies. Those who win the battles are our leaders and celebrities; those who fail are our losers and outcasts. Human services and many caring people function as stretcher-bearers for those who have fallen on the battlefield. In its crudest, implicit rendering this paradigm comes down to: conquer or die. In short, the politics of war and injustice function as the implicate paradigm shaping our consciousness, and thereby the way we relate to each other and the world.

Our glorification of the autonomous individual at the expense of the well-being of the whole has thrown our culture out of balance. In part, this glorification represents an immature rendering of the hero myth, which is a foundational archetype shaping Western consciousness. A mature, balanced consciousness would see the journey of the hero as an *inward quest* for self-awareness; instead, our culture has distorted its meaning into a call to an *outer conquest* over a hostile world.

The victims of this outer conquest are those who are deemed weaker or inferior because of the color of their skin, and an unruly natural world that must be controlled according to our will. The hero as the bearer of light to a darkened world becomes perverted into a conqueror over outer circumstances, resulting in a kind of Social Darwinism, in which the mighty prevail and the weak ones who fall by the wayside deserve their fate due to inherent flaws in their character.

Like Old Mouse, those in positions of power attempt to instill fear of an "evil" world in us and then tempt us with promises of wealth, security, democracy, knowledge, and salvation—as long as we toe the line. At the level of pure survival, they are simply exploiting a natural tendency in all of us to want to possess material security as a hedge against poverty and death. This is illustrated in the story "Gluscabi and the Game Animals" that comes out of the Abenaki tradition in the Northeast. A shortened version of the story follows:

> Whenever Gluscabi went hunting, the animals hid from him.
> He became frustrated and devised a scheme to trick them. But
> first he had Grandmother Woodchuck make a game bag for him.
> Grandmother Woodchuck made the first game bag out of caribou
> hair. But Gluscabi didn't like it and demanded she make another
> one. She made another game bag out of deer hair and again he
> didn't like it. The next game bag she made out of moose hair and
> the same thing happened. Finally, Grandmother Woodchuck made

a game bag out of the hairs from her own belly. Now this game bag was magical: no matter how much you put into it, there would still be room for more. Gluscabi was pleased with it.

Now Gluscabi went to a clearing in the forest and called out as loud as he could, "All you animals, listen to me. A terrible thing is going to happen. The sun is going to go out. The world is going to end and everything is going to be destroyed."

Frightened the animals came to the clearing and asked Gluscabi what they could do to survive. He told them to just climb into his game bag and they would be safe.

So all the animals went into his game bag. Soon all the animals in the world were in Gluscabi's game bag. He tied it off and carried it back to Grandmother. "Grandmother," he said, "we no longer have to go out and walk around looking for food. Whenever we want anything to eat we can just reach into my game bag."

Grandmother was not pleased with what Gluscabi had done. She said, "Oh, Gluscabi, why must you always do things this way? You cannot keep all of the game animals in a bag. They will sicken and die. There will be none left for our children and our children's children. It is also right that it should be difficult to hunt them. Then you will grow stronger trying to find them. And the animals will also grow stronger and wiser trying to avoid being caught. Then things will be in the right balance."

Well, Gluscabi saw that Grandmother was right. So he carried the game bag back to the clearing in the forest and opened it up. "All you animals," he called, "you can come out now. Everything is all right. The world was destroyed, but I put it back together again."

Gluscabi illustrates a need for security and comfort that we all share. We all desire happiness and freedom from suffering. However, this natural desire can be perverted by fear and greed into actions that only increase our suffering. For instance, Gluscabi allows his dissatisfaction with the way things are to fan an insatiable greed that knows no limits and that would in time bring about the destruction of his world.

From a Buddhist perspective, the dissatisfaction that Gluscabi feels is the underlying condition of our human experience and the cause of our suffering. It is this dissatisfaction, often a barely perceptible current running beneath the busyness of our days, that gnaws at us and keeps us from being fully present in the moment and appreciative of what is right here before us right now. Instead of accepting things as they are, we are driven by a desire to change them in order to get what we want. This drive is the origin of the treadmill of suffering, which continually spins until we see through this unrelenting cycle of dissatisfaction and grasping.

Clearly, Gluscabi's greed has upset the balance of things, just as the greed of our culture threatens the ecological balance of the planet. It takes the wisdom of Grandmother—a genuine elder—to make him aware of the error of his ways. As Grandmother says, to maintain balance one must take only what one needs, and doing so will insure that there will be something left for future generations.

Her message is clear: We must not think only of ourselves, for we are part of a larger world, which also includes those who haven't been born yet. Each being within our world is interdependent with all the other beings, such that an injury to one impacts all of us. Wisdom is the recognition and honoring of this vast web of "interbeing," as the Buddhist monk Thich Nhat Hanh calls it.

Knowledge versus Wisdom

Old Mouse is the embodiment of the egoic mind's natural tendency to want to know everything. He is motivated by the partially correct assumption that knowledge will give him power to protect himself and control his world. However, Old Mouse has been lulled into a false sense of authority with respect to what he knows. He believes that his capacity to see and know the names of the animals of the Prairie gives him a special knowledge, indeed wisdom. But he is deluded.

From a mythological perspective, there are creation myths where naming things is equivalent to the power to create. An obvious example is to be found in Genesis: In the beginning there was the Word of God, and all of creation came into being through that Logos. Likewise, among the Aborigines of Australia, every feature of the land is given a name based on an event through which it first came into being in the Dreamtime, their creation myth.

But there is also a sense in which naming signifies merely a superficial knowledge. Krishnamurti, a lucid 20th-century teacher from India, said that once you tell a child the name of a tree, the tree is forever lost to the child. Once the child knows the name of the tree, the unmediated experience of the tree has been displaced by a concept. From then on, he will be unable to experience the tree in its immediacy, in its pure presence. The label replaces the miracle of the life form in front of him and creates a distance between the child and the tree. Once the child knows the name of a thing, he no longer pays attention to it; it becomes known and taken for granted, like the other known things of his world that he passes by each day without a second glance.

Old Mouse's naming falls into this category. Within the smugness of his knowing there is no room for further exploration, discovery, surprise, or mystery. His knowing is like a door closing on the world, whereas genuine knowing is like a door opening onto a vast, infinite world—the mystery of life itself.

From this perspective, the type of naming demonstrated by Old Mouse signifies a conventional knowledge that comes with our capacity to know the names and uses of things. This naming of things is, of course, necessary and useful for the purposes of communication and industry.

Taken to its highest expression such knowledge is equivalent to the objective knowledge of the classical sciences and modern technology. It is rational, discursive, linear, and practical. It has produced many technological wonders, both beneficial and destructive, from the light bulb to the atom bomb. It has given us many comforts and luxuries that have enhanced the quality of our lives. At a material level, many people in our country live in a "haven."

But this type of knowledge is limited to special circumstances and does not take into account the full complexity of life. For instance, as quantum physics has revealed, light exhibits the qualities of both a particle and a wave, so it is impossible to designate it as one or the other. In one instance, it behaves like a particle, in another like a wave. So the new sciences are revealing that there is a complexity and ambiguity to life that defies simplistic classifications. The new sciences are opening a door onto mystery.

Moreover, this objective knowledge has definite limitations. While it may serve our practical needs it does not meet our spiritual needs, and thus does not qualify as wisdom. Wisdom moves beyond the practical to the matters of the heart and Spirit. Objective knowledge alone is ultimately empty and soulless. Old Mouse may know the names of things, but he hasn't been *touched* by them in his heart, because his worldview places a wall between himself and the Other. This wall of objectification, behind which he has secured himself, precludes the possibility of forming a relationship with the Other. Thus, he will never truly know the beings that he can name, leaving him forever lonely.

On the other hand, wisdom reveals itself as a *gnosis,* a knowing that penetrates below the surface of things to the underlying soul of what is perceived. Gnosis comes as a revelation, a gift of the imagination. From the depths of its interiority, a being or thing reveals itself and in the same moment conceals itself, retreating back into its depths, into what is ineffable. In this view, no thing can be known in its entirety; it always dances on the edge of mystery. Also, in bearing witness to this disclosure and concealment within the flame of attention, one's own self is revealed. A poem by Rainer Maria Rilke gives expression to this way of perceiving:

The Way In

Whoever you are: some evening take a step
out of your house, which you know so well.
Enormous space is near, your house lies where it begins,
whoever you are.
*   Your eyes find it hard to tear themselves*
from the sloping threshold, but with your eyes
slowly, slowly, lift one black tree
up, so it stands against the sky: skinny, alone.
*   With that you have made the world. The world is immense*
and like a word that is still growing in the silence.
*   In the same moment that your will grasps it,*
your eyes, feeling its subtlety, will leave it...
—*RAINER MARIA RILKE, THE BOOK OF PICTURES*

Venturing outside the house he knows so well, the poet bears witness to the beauty and wonder evoked by a simple tree. For the poet, this tree stands on the threshold of time and eternity, the known and the unknown, the word and silence, and speaks of an immensity that can barely be grasped or spoken: "The world is immense and like a word that is still growing in the silence." This simple tree speaks to the poet's heart of a vast ensouled world, a living organic whole, infinite in its interconnections—ultimately ungraspable in its totality, yet at the same time radiant in its implications and beauty.

This moment of witnessing is a revelation, a gnosis that reveals the sacredness of life and that transforms the seer. Although such a moment may be experienced as a heightened awareness, it is at the same time as ordinary as drinking a glass of cold water on a hot day. And like the glass of water, it refreshes and enlivens. When one slows down enough to bring this quality of attention to each moment, each moment carries the imprint of eternity and fills our lives with appreciation and gratitude.

As a poet, Rilke was completely taken up with the project of naming the utterly ordinary things of life, and through these acts of "transforming attention" of bearing witness to their sacredness. This is a naming, an act of imagination, that is foreign to the experience of Old Mouse. Having steeled his heart behind the armor of objective knowing, he has cut himself off from the source of imagination and a knowing that arises out of the living nexus of relationship. In Rilke's naming he was approaching a God who was once immanent in the things of the world, as in the pre-Christian pagan consciousness, but who had been removed from the world of things by the tendency of institutionalized religion to place God in some remote transcendent realm.

When addressing this former God in his *Book of Hours*, Rilke writes, " ... I want to portray you not with lapis or gold, but with colors made of apple bark.... I want, then, simply to say the name of things" (I,60). And, again, later in his life in the ninth *Duino Elegy*, Rilke writes that through the simple act of naming the ordinary things of our lives-" house, bridge, well, jug, fruit tree, window"- we are rescuing them from their obscurity and transience, and at the same moment delivering ourselves from our own transience.

Such naming, which in its essence is an act of perceiving, springs from a touching and being touched that moves within the orbit of seer and seen, and that is informed by a profound experience of the oneness of all things. This relational orbit amounts to a two-way energetic exchange, as energy moves from the seer to the seen, and from the seen to the seer. Within the orbit of this touching, ordinary things are lifted out of their obscurity into a clearing, where they blaze forth with the shining presence of the holy.

In Rilke's poetry, it is as though God comes into view most clearly through simple acts of communion with the things of the world. In an awareness of a kinship and shared fate with the things of the world, poet and subject become mirrors to each other, revealing the hidden, vital connection of spirit between them. Here, consciousness and its accompanying awareness of mortality, instead of driving a wedge of arrogance between humans and the other beings of the world, creates a psychic/energetic bridge across the threshold between worlds.

It is precisely in this ecstatic experience of kinship and oneness that the sacredness of life becomes manifest. It is when one is able to stand outside one's self—the root of ecstacy, *ek-stasis*, literally means outside the rational, conditioned, fearful, self-centered, separate self—that the magnificent splendor of the Universe unfolds before our eyes and speaks to us in ten thousand and one tongues of glory.

The modern disconnection from a vibrant, interdependent, ensouled world has made such experiences increasingly rare and undervalued when they do occur. These experiences of kinship and oneness with the natural world, however, were the norm in our human experience among indigenous peoples and Goddess-worshipping pagans for tens of thousands of years prior to the life-negating tendencies within patriarchal religious systems and scientific rationalism.

These feelings of intimate connectedness are still a part of our experience today, and not just for poets. Perhaps you have experienced being drawn fully into the present moment, your attention captured beyond time, by witnessing the bubbling joy of an infant, the shining innocence in a child's face, the exquisite beauty of a sunset or mountain vista, the utter peace of being entwined within your lover's embrace, the comfortable silence between old friends, the suffering or death of a loved one, and so on.

These experiences of oneness are primary, primal, potent, healing, transformative, and ultimately evolutionary. They are real, and the disconnection is unreal. As the cultural historian William Irwin Thompson writes,

> We have to use the "Imagination" to recover a sense of the sacred. The sacred is the emotional force which connects the part to the whole; the profane or secular is that which has been broken off from, or has fallen off, its emotional bond to the universe. *Religare* means to bind up, and the traditional task of religion has been to bind up the pieces that have broken away from the ecstatic Oneness.

True religion reconnects the individual with an awe-inspiring sense of the greater whole—the holiness of the Universe. In our modern world, however, where traditional religions have failed to fulfill this role, we must turn for inspiration to spiritual traditions and the poets and artists and mystics who haven't lost this primal connection to a sacred Earth.

The archetypal poet within us sings the world into existence as though it were born anew in each moment. We sing with the mythic, primordial voice of the indigenous soul that issues forth from the heartbeat of the Earth. This voice sings one thing in ten thousand and one different ways: *I belong on the Earth; I am of the Earth; all creatures are my brothers and sisters; I am grateful for this life.*

This mythopoeic consciousness was and, in some cases, is the norm among indigenous people. For instance, among the Mayans, it was said that the Otherworld sings all of creation into being. Each living being is its song, and we return the favor by singing our gratitude in prayers and songs. Similarly, in the Dreamtime of the Aboriginals of Australia, the Ancestors created the world by singing it into existence. These creation myths convey the original sense of *poeisis*, to create through speaking.

In the Dreamtime, each Ancestor—each of whom corresponds to one of the myriad things that make up the world—emerged at a particular place on the land and had a singular Dreaming associated with it. Correlatively, each Aboriginal has his or her own totemic animal and its corresponding place of origin, and thus his or her own unique Dreaming, which is expressed through song. When an Aboriginal goes on a Walkabout, he retraces the steps of an Ancestor and reenacts the original creation by singing the Dreaming associated with each landmark on the journey—the fabled "songlines" of the Aborigines. In this way, the primordial Dreamtime of the Ancestors is sung into the present.

What is significant in this mythic consciousness, as the scholar of comparative religion Mircea Eliade points out, is that the past—the original Time—is never lost;

rather it is continuously recreated in the present through rituals and gestures that have been done before. As Eliade puts it, "The gesture acquires meaning, reality, solely to the extent to which it repeats a primordial act." The reenactment of a primordial act through ritual unites time with an eternal present; it gives a sense of cosmic continuity within cyclical change. The eternal return of the same makes each moment sacred and roots the Aboriginal in the present and on Earth.

But we moderns are swept up and away by the rush of history—the chaos of unrepeatable, discontinuous, secular events with no inherent rhyme or reason. In our alienated world, it is the poetic, creative, or mythic sensibility, rooted in the indigenous soul within each of us, that feels and evokes this primordial state outside the meaningless sweep of time and history. It is this transfiguring feeling that brings us to care, create, build, forgive, sacrifice, and love again and again, in spite of the suffering that accompanies living.

This mythopoeic consciousness, which the archetypal psychologist James Hillman affirms as the "poetic basis of mind," is foreign to Old Mouse. His orientation to reality, tightly circumscribed by fear and a rigid need to be in control, maintains a chokehold on imagination. The Old Mouse in each of us clings to his favorite concepts and habits out of fear of the unknown, out of fear of not knowing; ultimately, out of fear of the great unknown that awaits each of us— death. We create and cling to our seemingly solid life rafts, like the mental construct of a separate self, in the shifting, ambiguous, infinite sea of life, not wishing to acknowledge that in the next moment our little raft could be turned upside down by a storm raging in our own hearts or in the world.

In contrast with Old Mouse, who refuses to budge from his haven, Jumping Mouse's journey moves him beyond the need to armor his heart with inherited, socially conditioned ways of perceiving and to learn to see with the eye of the heart from deep within the storms of life. The spirit of Jumping Mouse also lives within each of us. Each moment holds the choice of which one we want to feed: Old Mouse or Jumping Mouse.

Denial of the Quest

The shadow side of Old Mouse becomes most visible when he tells Jumping Mouse that "…the Great Mountains are only a myth. Forget your passion to see them and stay here with me." Old Mouse uses the word "myth" solely in the pejorative sense, as something that is not true, an illusion, or fanciful, just as it is used in common vernacular. His—and our—linear, literal rationality wars against the mythopoeic consciousness that informed the prehistoric life of humans on this planet for tens of thousands of years and gave birth to a sense of the sacred that played a critical role in the evolution of *Homo sapiens* from hominids. As Monica Sjoo and Barbara Mor contend in *The Great Cosmic Mother: Rediscovering the Religion of the Earth:*

> A sacramental bond between our earliest human ancestors and the natural world was the primary factor in our evolution—not simply as a physical species, but as conscious beings. For this bonding set up a resonance in which art, all religious ritual, all magic-alchemic science, all spiritual striving for illumination was born.

The life-renewing, life-affirming, life-celebratory, life-evolving significance of myth and ritual is lost to Old Mouse's dry, one-dimensional rational consciousness. Complacent within our knowing, we can, like Old Mouse, forget this realm. As the gods and goddesses retreat from our world, we are left with a de-animated world, and our days are haunted by an uneasy feeling of unreality and an inner emptiness.

The real task of the elder in today's world is to revive a sense of the *anima mundi*, the soul of the world, and then to tend it with care and love, like a fire upon which our survival depends. The critical task today is the resurrection of imagination from the fatal jaws of dualistic moralisms, religious fundamentalism, objective knowledge, and the conqueror mentality. Instead, Old Mouse is content to fill his belly and brag about his ability to name things.

When Old Mouse tells Jumping Mouse to forget his passion, he has become a voice of death, a living death, a soulless existence. His denial of the quest is equivalent to a denial of life itself. He is like the men and women in our lives who try to kill the spark of passion, longing, inspiration, and wonder (the child) in us, because they have drowned their own spark in the wake of their concessions to work, security, comfort, and conformity. In the abject bitterness and pain of their half-lived lives, they unconsciously try to bring down anyone who seeks to step outside the mold of conformity and mediocrity that they have succumbed to. In their silent despair, they suffer from the postmodern maladies of depression and detachment, ennui and hyperactivity, skepticism and cynicism.

A Contracted Emotional Body

Old Mouse has lost touch with the wonder, innocence, trust, unconditional love, imagination, and vital emotional body of the child. As children, raised in a "good enough" family, we play freely and joyfully "in the Fields of the Lord." In our innocence and trust, we live in a state of openness and wonder, attuned to the magic and mystery of a radiant world. As I've learned on our Vision Quest programs, many people have glimpses into the soul of the world during childhood—a feeling of a loving presence at the foot of their bed, a magical place in a forest where fairies dwell, a shining light that emanates from the beings around them, the sweet balm of unconditional love.

Imagination plays a critical role within the development of a child—indeed, within the evolution of human consciousness. Just as a child's body grows and stretches to new heights through the intake of food, so too a child's mind grows and stretches to new possibilities through the active exercise of imagination. Just as food energizes the body, so too imagination enlivens consciousness. In the world of imagination, things that have been separated by the limitations of ordinary consciousness are brought back together again into an integrated whole. In a child's imagination, there is no separation between the human world and the natural world; instead, they are woven together to form one enchanted tapestry of many different strands. Such a world is made of magic, where anything is possible.

Somehow as we age, we can lose the sense of wonder and magic of the child. As adults, we can become locked into assumed identities and characteristics that narrowly define who we are: doctor, teacher, carpenter, introvert, extrovert, depressed, angry, happy-go-lucky, failure, successful, powerful, victim, wounded, and so on. Our outlook on life can become rigidly limited by what we know to the extent that nothing new under the sun can enter our world. We also carry more of life's losses on our shoulders—the deaths of friends and loved ones, the abandoned dreams of our youth. Under the weight of responsibilities and losses, we can lose touch with the spirit of the child, or even reject that part of ourselves because it seemingly doesn't help us to earn a living, to become successful, to be somebody important, or to act like a responsible, mature adult.

Rejecting the child part of himself, Old Mouse has armored his emotional body, in fear of showing vulnerability, in fear of appearing weak, in fear of letting his despair rise to the surface. Although perhaps this condition is to be found more commonly in men, women are by no means exempt from it. Assuming the role of the rugged, autonomous individual tends to flatten our emotional life in such a way that we don't have access to the full range of our emotions. To truly feel would be dangerous (we rationalize), for then we might have to acknowledge the "quiet desperation" of our life, our rage against our father or mother, our self-doubts, our loneliness, our fears, our despair about the fate of the Earth, and so on. If we did that we might fall apart and never be able to put ourselves back together again. That's the fear anyway. So up comes the façade of control.

This fear of descending into and revealing the depths of our emotional life is conditioned and reinforced daily by a society that denies the value of an inner life, and, one might add, the reality of suffering and death. Mass media, religious and educational institutions, and even the mental health industry in its over-reliance on medications, drum this denial into our heads day after day.

Perhaps, from an early age, as a young girl, you were taught to be pleasant and cheerful and to accommodate yourself to the needs of others. Seeking the approval of others, you may have put on a social persona and forgot or denied who and what you truly are. Tragically, you may have drifted through life never feeling quite good enough and always feeling anxious, because how can you ever really know for certain if you are actually meeting someone else's expectations. As a young boy, you may have been pressured to grow up quickly; whenever you showed any kind of vulnerability, like fear or tears, you were told to act like a man. According to our cultural definition of masculinity, a real man is physically and emotionally strong, which is to say he shows little or no emotion, with the exception of anger. What this does to the soul and emotional life of men is devastating. It condemns men to a shrunken, hardened, lonely existence, because it dries up the emotional waters upon which a life rich in relationships is based. Hiding our interior life behind these social masks, we find it difficult to make any real contact with each other, and the juice of living gradually dries up.

Furthermore, the denial of our emotional life is reinforced by the primary value our culture places upon the development of our rational capabilities, at the expense of the heart. Even women, who stereotypically have greater access to their emotions, are not immune to the negative impact of this overemphasis upon reason. Through the exercise of rational will, the mind attempts to control our emotions through repression. Of course, repression doesn't work; it only reinforces the repressed emotions, which eventually will leak out in unhealthy, reactive ways. But this emphasis upon reason, at the expense of the heart, is a formidable impediment to realizing our full humanity.

To realize our full humanity—to awaken from the trance of separation— inevitably involves a descent into the darkness of the unconscious, where rejected or split-off parts of ourselves dwell. Exploring difficult emotions, like fear, shame, envy, hatred, possessiveness, greed, rage, and so on, becomes part of the process of realizing our true nature. If the shadow, as Jung calls it, is not looked at and worked with, again and again, then our quest can be colored by the desires and ambitions of the ego, which seeks to pad its spiritual resumé with lofty concepts, profound experiences, and renowned teachers.

Paradoxically, the shadow needs to be accepted for what it is, rather than rejected or denied. Through this process of acceptance, the unconscious control that the shadow exerts over us is gradually broken, thereby releasing for the sake of the spiritual path a tremendous amount of energy that had previously been diverted into the suppression of the shadow. Unearthing the shadow can often be an essential part of the process of finding the precious jewel of our true nature that has been buried beneath the mask of personality from the very beginning of the quest. Without this soul work, the precious jewel becomes an intellectual concept or an ideal that someone else represents, and thereby always remains just beyond our reach.

My friend Charlie's story illustrates the importance of including our emotional reality in our spiritual journey. After years of Zen Buddhist practice, he was able to sit on his cushion for hours, through retreat after retreat, and realize a quiet mind, but his practice had become dry and lifeless. When he meditated, all his dark emotional stuff would scurry away into the corners of the meditation hall, like cockroaches when you turn on a light in a room. Eventually Charlie saw that by avoiding these issues he was avoiding a part of himself. Soon after this realization, he left his practice and began the deep emotional work of looking at the wounds of his childhood that still haunted him. With this work, he felt a great liberation of his spirit and now has resumed a meditation practice with renewed enthusiasm and vitality.

The reader may recall that my story is somewhat similar to Charlie's. When I first took up meditation years ago, I unwittingly used it as a means to escape the pain of my life. Resting on this unconscious intention, my practice only succeeded in separating me farther from life. I retreated from active participation in the world to the spiritual position of the detached observer. This disengaged position allowed me to bypass my inner emotional reality; as a consequence, I was unable to embody my spirituality in everyday life. Eventually, through psychotherapy, especially a body-centered modality, I addressed the core wounds of a difficult childhood. Now, many years later, I have also resumed a meditation practice. But, based on this inner work, my practice has brought me more deeply into the heart of each moment and into relationship.

Body-centered psychotherapies, such as Core Energetics, Bioenergetics, Hakomi, Focusing, Somatic Experiencing, and EMDR (Eye Movement Desensitization and Reprocessing), have proven to be effective in treating deep-seated emotional wounds. As the pioneering psychologist Wilhelm Reich observed, the body is the unconscious, insofar as it is the frozen history of our past.

Emotional traumas are imprinted upon the cells of our body and manifest in areas of chronic pain and tension. When we focus upon the body through deep listening, breath, movement, and palpation, these areas of contraction begin to open up, releasing the deeply held emotions. Through this process, we gain access to an increasing *experiential* awareness, as opposed to a merely *conceptual* understanding, of the core patterns and beliefs that limit our full life expression. With this awareness we are able to disidentify with the old storylines and reactive patterns that have ruled us and to embody the light of our spirituality in our daily life. Life then becomes our practice and teacher.

The experiences of Charlie and myself notwithstanding, it needs to be stated that a meditation practice does not, in itself, necessarily promote an avoidance of difficult emotions. In fact, as the internal chatter of the mind settles down, meditation can be a powerful vehicle for allowing deep, unconscious material to bubble up to the surface where it can be fully felt and eventually transmuted as we learn to sit with it in a nonjudgmental and nonreactive way. What's most important is the intention of the practitioner and the orientation of the particular spiritual path he or she is following.

The steely mask of invulnerability and cool rational control that our society holds up as an ideal standard of behavior is a sham of strength, a straw man bound to fall apart when faced with real adversity. Real strength and power derives from our capacity to be authentically human, acknowledging both our weaknesses and our strengths.

A Failure of Imagination

Old Mouse, as the mouthpiece of egoic consciousness, has sealed himself off from Nature; in fact, Nature has become an enemy—no, *the* enemy. With his defensive structures rigidly in place, very little of the vibrant miracle of life is able to penetrate deeply. His rigidity is in place to prevent any natural impulses or errant flights of imagination from taking control of him, for he must always be in control. To lose control is to lose his sense of self, for his self is completely identified with being in control. In fact, being in control takes on the guise of a moral imperative, and this quasi-moral imperative is directed against an unruly, messy Nature, both inside and outside.

In this, we hear echoes of Western civilization's protracted battle to tame the beast within, which was inaugurated by the Church and later given its stamp of quasi-scientific approval by Freud. The tragedy is, however, that as we encapsulate ourselves within fear-based cocoons of defensiveness, and outer walls of steel, concrete, and missile defense systems, we are removing ourselves more completely from the heart-beat of the Earth. This emotional and imaginative disconnection has led to what the visionary cultural historian Thomas Berry describes, in a chilling assessment, as a kind of "autism": a psychic withdrawal from the natural world, a numbing to the pain of another, and a preoccupation with virtual reality. A people this far removed from reality, this hardened and disconnected, are in critical danger of self-destructing.

In the end, Old Mouse represents a failure of imagination. The opposite of the self-centered, rigid mind of Old Mouse is an awakened mind—a mind steeped in the power of imagination, vision, and compassion. The power of imagination resides in its capacity to see through the ordinary things of the world to their inner core and to see relationships of interdependency where none are apparent.

The wings of imagination carry us beyond the ego's preoccupation with survival, comfort, and control to a place where we can be touched by the beauty and mystery of a radiant world. It is imagination that can carry us back into the heart of Nature and the world. Imagination unites and gives us the capacity to enter into the experience of the Other. Imagination and vision shape the heart into an organ of compassion and transformation. Imagination and vision—the wings of Eagle—lift humanity into the higher potentials of human consciousness.

Through some ordinary miracle Jumping Mouse knows this and is not tempted by the promises of security and comfort offered by Old Mouse. Instead, he is resolved to travel farther into the possibilities he senses within himself. As my teacher, Steven Foster, used to say, he has entered "decision road"—he has embodied the quest.

In sum, Old Mouse exists in each of us. He is the part of us that resists change, that clings to our old attitudes, beliefs, judgments, and wounds as a shield against letting any new possibilities enter our lives. He represents that part of us that views reality through a lens of fear and that clings to material reality for dear life. Old Mouse's fear hides behind masks of rationality, control, emotional coolness, busyness, depression, judgment, critique, analysis, self-righteousness, superiority, all-knowingness, perfectionism, and conformity. His function is to silence the voice of the soul—the small, quiet voice of intuition, imagination, and the heart. He is afraid of and violently opposed to anything that is wild, free, and holy, for it threatens the very basis of his control. It threatens the very definition of himself and the world.

Buffalo:

The Spirit of the Give-Away

*A human being is a part of the whole called by us Universe, a part
limited in time and space. He experiences himself, his thoughts and
feelings as something separated from the rest, a kind of optical delusion
of his consciousness. This delusion is a kind of prison for us, restricting
us to our personal desires and to affection for a few persons nearest to
us. Our task must be to free ourselves from this prison by widening our
circle of compassion to embrace all living creatures and the whole of
nature in its beauty.*

—*ALBERT EINSTEIN*

It was hard for Jumping Mouse to leave, but he gathered his determination and ran hard again. The ground was rough. But he arched
his tail and ran with all his might. He could feel the shadows of the
spots upon his back as he ran. All those spots!

Finally he ran into a stand of chokecherries. Jumping Mouse
could hardly believe his eyes. It was cool there and very spacious.
There was water, cherries and seeds to eat, grasses to gather for
nests, holes to be explored and many, many other busy things to do.
And there were a great many things to gather.

He was investigating his new domain when he heard very heavy
breathing. He quickly investigated the sound and discovered its
source. It was a great mound of hair with black horns. It was a great
buffalo. Jumping Mouse could hardly believe the greatness of the
being he saw lying there before him. He was so large that Jumping
Mouse could have crawled into one of his great horns.

"Such a magnificent being," thought Jumping Mouse, and he
crept closer. "Hello, my brother," said Jumping Mouse.

"Why are you lying here?"

"I am sick and dying," Buffalo said, "And my medicine has told me that only the eye of a mouse can heal me. But little brother, there is no such thing as a mouse."

Jumping Mouse was shocked. "One of my eyes!" he thought. "One of my tiny eyes." He scurried back into the stand of choke-cherries. But the breathing came harder and slower.

"He will die," thought Jumping Mouse, "if I do not give him my eye. He is too great a being to let die."

He went back to where the Buffalo lay and spoke. "I am a mouse," he said with a shaky voice. "And you, my brother, are a great being. I cannot let you die. I have two eyes, so you may have one of them."

The minute he said it, Jumping Mouse's eye flew out of his head and Buffalo was made whole. Buffalo jumped to his feet, shaking Jumping Mouse's whole world.

"Thank you, my little brother," said Buffalo. "I know of your quest for the Sacred Mountains and of your visit to the river. You have given me life so that I may Give-Away to The People. I will be your brother forever. Run under my belly and I will take you right to the foot of the Sacred Mountains, and you need not fear the spots. The eagles cannot see you while you run under me.

All they will see will be the back of a buffalo. I am of the Prairie and I will fall on you if I try to go up the mountains."

Little Mouse ran under the Buffalo, secure and hidden from the spots, but with only one eye it was frightening. The Buffalo's great hooves shook the whole world each time he took a step. Finally they came to a place and Buffalo stopped.

"This is where I must leave you, little brother," said Buffalo.

"Thank you very much," said Jumping Mouse. "But you know, it was very frightening running under you with only one eye. I was constantly in fear of your great earth-shaking hooves."

"Your fear was for nothing," said Buffalo. "For my way of walking is the Sun Dance Way, and I always know where my hooves will fall. I now must return to the Prairie, my brother. You can always find me there."

It may be hard for Jumping Mouse to leave the comfortable and secure life that Old Mouse offers him. But he does. The "holy longing" within him is too strong to be tempted by that life. Somewhere within each of us a similar longing burns, and each of us has the capacity to respond by turning toward it. Our potential for transformation is a seed within our hearts awaiting this inward turn. The decision is ours—whether to venture forth into the unknown, or to remain hidden, like Old Mouse, never venturing out of our safe, insulated cocoon, fearing the unknown possibilities within ourselves, yet forever plagued by an unsettling, barely conscious hunger for something more in our lives. Many people today find themselves in this limbo place of material plenty but inner emptiness.

So Jumping Mouse gathers his determination and sets off again deeper into the Prairie. The going is rough and he feels the shadows of the eagles on his back, but he moves deeper into the unknown that stretches before him. When he stops to rest in a stand of chokecherries, a place that even surpasses the Old Mouse's haven, he comes upon a buffalo whose breathing is labored. Upon inquiry he learns that Buffalo is sick and dying and that only the eye of a mouse will heal him. "But little brother," Buffalo says, "there is no such thing as a mouse."

Buffalo's ignorance of the existence of a mouse gives Jumping Mouse a perfect opportunity to remain hidden and to withdraw from the challenge presented to him. Remaining incognito, he could have waited for Buffalo to die and then taken over this beautiful stand of chokecherries for his home. Of course, then, he would have to smell the rotting flesh of Buffalo and be constantly reminded of his failure to respond to the suffering of another being.

Jumping Mouse is understandably shocked by the choice presented to him. To give up one of his eyes is not an easy thing to do. But Jumping Mouse reasons that he cannot let such a magnificent being die, if he possesses the medicine to heal him. And, ultimately, each of us possesses the medicine to heal another; it comes in the form of compassion.

After thinking it over awhile, Jumping Mouse decides to sacrifice one of his eyes so that Buffalo may live. Etymologically, the word "sacrifice" comes from the Latin *sacrificum*, which is composed of two words: *sacer*, meaning holy, sacred, and *facere*, meaning to do, to make. Sacrifice, therefore, means "to make holy." Thus this momentous decision places Jumping Mouse firmly on holy ground.

In sacrificing one of his eyes, Jumping Mouse is sacrificing a mouse way of perceiving the world. He is letting go of some habitual, conditioned mouse way of thinking, feeling, and acting. Although Jumping Mouse is on a quest, he is still attached to a material, egocentric view of reality. Inhabiting such a one-dimensional world, in which greed and self-interest prevail, condemns him to a life of mistrust as he battles against other mice for food and security. In other words, from a purely material perspective, it is absolutely absurd to give up one of your eyes. We need our eyes to make our way in the world and to watch out for approaching dangers. To sacrifice an eye is to compromise our ability to survive.

So Jumping Mouse's decision to sacrifice an eye takes place on a plane of existence other than the merely material. His decision stems from an underlying, although at this point only partially formed, sense that there is something more to life than just material satisfaction and security. His act of sacrifice is a prefiguring of the new spiritual way of perceiving reality that has been growing within him; indeed, the act itself is already an example of this new orientation.

At this stage in his journey Jumping Mouse does not know that, paradoxically, the loss of an eye will actually improve his vision—his vision into the true nature of self and reality. His sacrifice is an act of pure trust and innocence, with no self-serving attachment to how it may benefit him. His selfless act, pure and simple, is a response to the suffering of another being.

But how is it that an eye of a little mouse will heal a great being like Buffalo?

Buffalo is the embodiment of the spirit of the Give-Away. Among the Plains Indians, the Give-Away signifies an original instruction of Nature that encompasses the whole spectrum of life from the purely physical plane to the spiritual. On the physical plane, an animal gives away his life so that another may live; and, then, as the great circle of life revolves, the predator becomes prey for another animal, and so on and so on. A higher expression of the Give-Away is to be found in the unconditional love and selfless care that parents, human or nonhuman, give to their offspring. On an even higher level, extending the selflessness of the parent beyond the family, a native person sacrifices his or her own self-interests in order to serve the well-being of the whole tribe. In another profound expression of the Give-Away, if a native person feels that his material possessions are getting in the way of his relationship to Great Spirit, he puts all of his belongings, from blankets to horses, out in front of his house and asks his relatives and friends to come over and take what they need. Clearly, the self-centeredness of Old Mouse is the antithesis of the Give-Away.

Within the great circling of life, Buffalo gives away the ultimate sacrifice of his own life, so that The People of the Plains may live; every part of his body was used, going toward feeding, clothing, and housing The People. For the Plains Indians, Buffalo was *the* most sacred being, charged with *wakan* (holiness). The spirit of the Give-Away that he embodied served as a spiritual North Star for them. Because their daily lives were so dependent on Buffalo, both physically and spiritually, Buffalo may be understood as a mirror of The People themselves. The great herds of buffalo and the Plains tribes mirrored each other in their nomadic roaming across the Plains and in their qualities of endurance and courage before the fierce storms of winter.

Thus, the fate of Buffalo and The People are intertwined. So the fact that Buffalo is sick and dying is a very serious matter, since not only the physical health of The People is in jeopardy but also their spiritual health. The story says that just as Buffalo lies sick and dying, so do The People. Given the magnitude of what is at stake, the story says that The People can only be healed by an act of sacrifice or Give-Away comparable to that of Buffalo.

On the Medicine Wheel, Buffalo and the spirit of the Give-Away, as the orientation of the true elder, dwell in the North. But the power of the North in its fulfillment rests on the South—the place of the trust and innocence of a child. The true elder always maintains a connection with the innocence and wonder of the child. Within this view, in order to manifest the beauty of the Give-Away, you must transcend the fear of egoic consciousness that life will not give you what is needed to live and open yourself in trust to a gifting Earth.

As you put down your protective shield and surrender to Spirit, you awaken to the wonder and openness of the child. Needless to say, such a way wars against our deepest instinct for survival, yet it moves us beyond conquest consciousness toward the highest potential of human consciousness.

From this perspective, the integration of the adult (North) with the child (South) forms the central axis around which the Medicine Wheel turns and the foundation for community. The strength and wisdom necessary to build a strong, healthy community—a community in which each individual's primary concern is for the good of the whole—is rooted in the trusting heart of the child, a heart that trusts the basic goodness in humans.

Eschewing the fiction of a separate self that is independent of others, such a heart expands outward to form a nexus of vital interconnection and interdependence with other beings. Such selfless trust creates an unbounded openness to the infinite tendrils of relationship that already exist in the world. Within such a vibrant, ensouled, interactive web of touching, each being's life is inseparably intertwined with the welfare of the whole, such that if one being suffers, all suffer.

It is only in a world based on such trust that balance and harmony can be realized. Within the embrace of this trust, the individual and the world can be made whole—that is, holy. In the absence of such trust, communities become demoralized and fragmented into isolated families and alienated individuals as in our society. Such communities are floundering in a state of chaos and confusion, rooted in the trance of separateness. Of course, this situation is not a new story nor singular to our society; it has been repeated in many different societies throughout the course of history.

Nonetheless, the time is ripe for a radical reorientation as we become aware that the materialistic, self-aggrandizing, consumption-driven principles that currently prevail within our society have led to destabilizing social injustices and have taken us to the brink of ecological crisis.

In the end, if we are to survive our current social and ecological crisis, we must liberate the trusting heart from the trance of separateness. Such a heart always seeks to align itself with what is life-affirming, and with the fundamental sacredness of life, despite the all-too-many negative instances that threaten to undermine that trust. It is only such a heart that can truly bring about transformation at an individual and collective level.

In light of these considerations, Jumping Mouse's medicine is based on his capacity to trust and, correlatively, to take risks. On the banks of the Great River he takes a great leap of faith, and later he sets off on the journey to the Sacred Mountains. His medicine derives from his courage (from the Latin cor, meaning heart) and his resolve to venture forth into the unknown, to leap into the dark. His willingness to risk leaping into the unknown that permeates each moment of existence, from birth to death, bestows upon Jumping Mouse the Medicine Power to heal—to heal himself and The People, who are sick and dying.

Within the archetypal dynamic of the story, the healing of Jumping Mouse is inseparably connected with the healing of The People. In other words, Jumping Mouse heals himself through self-sacrifice for the benefit of the Other. Thus, the story says, Medicine Power derives from one's willingness to surrender to the heart-centered urgings of Spirit that, beyond fear and control, lift away the veils that separate us from each other and open our hearts in compassion to the cries of the world.

But why are Buffalo and The People sick and dying?

There are two layers to this dying. First, on the physical plane, The People cannot live if their primary source of food is dying away, which was a sad historical reality as white men wantonly exterminated the herds in an effort to destroy the Plains Indians. The spirit of The People drained out of them as the blood of Buffalo stained the Plains.

Second, on the spiritual plane, the dying of Buffalo symbolically foreshadows the death of the spirit of the Give-Away within the heart of The People, which in essence represents the spiritual death of The People. Buffalo lies on the verge of death because The People have forgotten the Give-Away. Under the pressure of the whites' expansion into their land, Indians were forced to go on the warpath and to forget the teachings of the Medicine Wheel and the Give-Away. Their hearts became hard as they struggled for survival against an unrelenting enemy who conducted war in a manner totally foreign to them. Heretofore, in intertribal battles the intention had never been to exterminate the other tribe from the face of the Earth. Although lives were definitely lost, the greatest honor was bestowed upon a warrior who "counted coup"—to touch or strike an unhurt man and to leave him alive—and this was frequently done. Whites, on the other hand, sought to completely annihilate the Indians, whom they regarded as inferior beings, undeserving of any mercy, since they were less than human.

Within our own time, when we greedily consume the body of the Earth without limit and cling to our material possessions, ideas, self-importance, resentments, and judgments—all the things that reinforce the trance of separateness—and forget the sacred interdependence of life and our own potential for creative change, we become sick and live closer to death than to life.

We become sick because we have lost a spiritual connection to the source of life, the Great River, the ever-flowing, ever-renewing, ever-evolving creative energy of the Universe. We become sick because we take the gifts of Mother Earth for granted, without prayers of gratitude and without giving something back to her in return. We become sick because we have forgotten our sacred connection to the Great Mystery that informs the web of life.

In our time of social and ecological imbalances, wisdom would be to embrace the spirit of the Give-Away—the spirit of care, trust, and self-sacrifice. The spirit of the Give-Away draws all beings together as brothers and sisters within an infinitely expanding, relational circle of care and love, like the expanding concentric rings formed by a stone dropped into a lake. The spirit of the Give-Away flows like a river from which all may drink and be renewed.

Once the spirit of the Give-Away has been restored in the hearts of The People, they will be made whole as one being walking the way of sacrifice, balance, and harmony—like Buffalo. This is the Way of Vision, of seeing with the eye of the heart into the reality of our interdependence and oneness. What flew out of Jumping Mouse's head to Buffalo was not only one of his eyes but also his heart. Buddhist scripture describes this awakening of compassion in the following way: "the heart *quivers* in response to the suffering of another being."

Buffalo is instantly healed by the care displayed in Jumping Mouse's selfless sacrifice. The healing power of the Give-Away is truly miraculous and its repercussions are infinite in reach. Whenever we break through the fear and self-centeredness that normally enshroud our hearts by performing acts of generosity and compassion, these qualities become stronger in us and in those touched by them, and the world moves closer to balance and harmony.

Knowing of his journey to the Sacred Mountains, Buffalo, in gratitude, offers to take him to the foothills of these mountains. So Jumping Mouse runs under his belly where he is shielded from the eagles. When they reach the foothills, Jumping Mouse informs Buffalo that he was very frightened that one of his great hooves would land on him and crush him. In response, Buffalo tells him that he had no reason to be afraid: "For my way of walking is the Sun Dance Way, and I always know where my hooves will fall."

Since the Sun Dance Way informs the way of seeing in this story, I will present a brief sketch of the Sun Dance, drawing from *The Sacred Pipe: Black Elk's Account of the Seven Rites of the Oglala Sioux.* I can also provide firsthand observations, since I had the great honor of attending a Lakota Sun Dance as a supporter for a friend who has been dancing for many years. For four days, I witnessed this sacred ceremony that had been performed annually on the Great Plains for hundreds of years before the U.S. government outlawed it in the late 1800s in an effort to demoralize the Indians. Today, it is no longer outlawed, no doubt because the abjectly poor and demoralized Indians are no longer seen as a threat.

The Sun Dance was given to a member of the Oglala Lakota in a vision and is the first and foremost sacred ceremony among the Sioux and other American Indian tribes. It is performed in many different locations, usually around the summer solstice, when the sun stands still at the most northern point of its ecliptic course. The heart of the Sun Dance is selfless sacrifice, "so that The People may live."

A cottonwood tree, which has received the prayers of a medicine man for a year, is cut down ceremonially without letting the branches touch the ground. It is brought to the dancing ground, festooned with colorful prayer flags attached to it by all the participants, and then placed upright in a hole in the center of a circle formed by a perimeter arbor. The dancing ground circle, which is open to the sun, becomes a physical representation of all of creation and is laid out according to the four sacred directions of the Medicine Wheel. The tree in the center represents Great Spirit, the sacred Mystery upon which all life depends.

Obvious analogies can be made to the universal symbol of the Tree of Life, which forms the central axis of the world and represents the center of transformation, where Heaven and Earth come together. As Carl Jung writes: "In the history of symbols this tree is described as the way of life itself, growing into that which eternally is and does not change; which springs from the union of opposites and, by its eternal presence, also makes that union possible."

An example of the Tree of Life, which bears striking similarities to the Sun Dance tree, can be found in Norse mythology. In the epic Old Norse poem *Poetic Edda,* the world tree Yggdrasil is a great ash tree that grows from the well of wisdom and extends over the entire Earth. The poem tells the tale of Odin, the highest god and creator of the cosmos and man, who hung on this tree for nine days and sacrificed his left eye, in order to gain the wisdom represented in the runes. So here we also see the theme of the sacrifice of an eye on the spiritual quest. Indeed, the theme of sacrifice occurs in all high religions. We need only think of the sacrifice of Christ on the wooden cross, where the cross is a substitute for the World Tree uniting the horizontal and vertical planes of existence—Earth and Heaven, respectively.

From a native perspective, the cottonwood tree in the Sun Dance also serves as a mirror of humanity. Humans raise up their arms in prayer to, and longing for, Great Spirit, and are rooted in the Earth. The sun dancers ritually enact this sacred connection between humanity and Spirit. Men and women, who are fasting and going without water, dance and pray before this sacred tree in the blazing summer sun for four days, as singers sing and drum. The constant beat of the drum, together with the dancing, praying, and fasting, can transport the dancers into an ecstatic state of rapport with Great Spirit.

The dancers focus their attention continually upon the tree as the symbol of Great Spirit. They are connected to the tree by an invisible cord that penetrates deep into their hearts. Among the Sioux, the dancers at some point make this invisible cord visible. The dancers' flesh is pierced ceremonially with the wing bone of an eagle through their chests, backs, or arms. Then, a rope that had been tied midway up the tree before it was raised upright is attached to the eagle bone. The dancers, keeping the rope taut, are connecting their bodies to "the thongs of Great Spirit which come down to Earth." They are making an offering of their flesh, of their self-importance and self-centered ways, to Great Spirit for the sake of The People.

Here, the great Oglala Lakota visionary and healer Black Elk reports the rationale for the dance as offered by the man to whom the Sun Dance was given in a vision:

> When we go to the center of the hoop [the center tree] we shall all cry, for we should know that anything born into this world which you see about you must suffer and bear difficulties. We are now going to suffer at the center of the sacred hoop, and by doing this may we take upon ourselves much of the suffering of our people.

Although many Westerners, myself included, are made squeamish by the piercing and all too easily condemn it as barbaric, certainly an analogy to the most hallowed image in Christendom—Christ on the cross—cannot be avoided. The Sun Dancers are pierced so that they "may take upon themselves much of the suffering of the people," just as Christ sacrificed his life in order to redeem the sins or suffering of the people. The intense suffering that a sun dancer undergoes is a measure of the humbling force needed to break through the tenacious self-centeredness of the ego.

The suffering of the dancers—dancing in the summer heat without water or food, piercing their flesh, and eventually breaking free by pulling on the ropes—humbles them before Great Spirit and their community. Their pain softens their warrior hearts and allows them to experience a connection with all beings who suffer, in particular with the more vulnerable and weak members of their own tribe. Their suffering teaches them compassion by breaking open their hearts.

To say that Sun Dancers dance "so that The People may live" means that The People may live only when the individual members of the tribe care about each other as brothers and sisters in identification with each person's suffering and in the spirit of the Give-Away. Without this Way of Care, the integrity and well-being of the tribe will crumble. The dance teaches the dancers to let go of their arrogance, attachments, and defenses—all the attributes and behaviors that separate one person from another. As Black Elk says, "This truth of the oneness of all things we understand a little better by participating in this rite, and by offering ourselves as a sacrifice."

This same sentiment is expressed in a critical passage in Storm's epic *Seven Arrows*. At an extremely dangerous time, when Indians were being attacked by encroaching whites and were torn between two opposing paths—the warpath and the Way of the Medicine Wheel—two braves visited an elder who possessed Great Medicine and asked him what his medicine was. He said:

> My greatest Medicine is One of the Mind, the Body, and the Heart. If you have One Hundred People who Live Together, and if Each One Cares for the Rest, there is One Mind. The Power of this One Single Mind is a Great One, and is a means of Keeping Sickness from Among them. If there are But One or Two Among them who Hate, there is little Threat to Any of the Hundred. But if Ten of that Hundred do not Care for the Rest of their Brothers and Sisters, then there is a Threat…
>
> The Threat is One of Sickness. …*Not caring for one another has always caused sickness among a People.* [my own italics]

By this standard, American society is clearly in deep trouble.

The Sun Dance that I witnessed was a magnificent ceremony whose profound beauty and pathos lifted the veil across my heart that separates the profane from the sacred. Of many memorable moments two stand out: the Sunrise Ceremony and going to the tree myself.

In the chilly dawn of the Sunrise Ceremony, male and female dancers dressed in beautiful skirts symbolizing the feminine part of themselves and their willingness to surrender their will to Great Spirit gathered outside the dancing circle and slowly entered in procession to the beating drums. Then, turning to the east as one body, the dancers and singers greeted the rising sun with a beautiful song. The beauty of this song pierced my heart and my tears flowed. What a beautiful ritual! To greet the new dawn as a community, with a song of thanksgiving to *Wakan Tanka*—how my heart longed for such a communal ritual of gratitude in my own life.

The third day of the dance was designated a healing day, during which a nondancer could offer prayers at the sacred tree after making a flesh sacrifice. Small pieces of skin are cut from your arm with a razor blade and then wrapped in a prayer bundle, which you tie to the tree.

As I stood at the edge of the dancing ground making a flesh sacrifice, my sun dancer friend, who was resting in the arbor with the other dancers, happened to see me and came over to escort me to the tree, according to ritual protocol. This was an amazing moment. Before the dance, Tom had talked about taking me to the tree and how special that would be for him, since I was the brother of his dearest friend who had died many years before. I had said that it would be special for me as well in remembrance of the spirit of my brother. And here it was happening, spontaneously.

My legs were weak as I walked out to the tree, and I sobbed openly. The power of the moment was like nothing I had ever felt before. My gaze was fixed on the tree as I looked up into its branches, which stretched upward to a brilliant blue sky and danced in the wind, along with the many prayer flags. I felt the power of Great Spirit surge through me. When we reached the tree, I tied my sacrifice to it and prayed. I prayed my heart out, words and tears flowing together in gratitude and surrender.

The Sun Dance is a powerful and beautiful ceremony that ritually and dramatically enacts our connection to Spirit through a willingness to endure suffering for the sake of the greater whole. But even though I feel the utmost respect for the Sun Dance and the dancers, I must say that to walk the way of the Sun Dance one does not have to become a sun dancer.

Our suffering and longings are "the piercings in the flesh" that unite us to the divine, for they can humble us and initiate the quest that leads to the Sacred Mountains. It is these piercings that open the heart to the mystery of life and death, and stir the embers of compassion. Indeed, to walk the way of the Sun Dance it is enough to set one's intention to walk the Way of Care, to live in accord with Nature, and to surrender one's heart to the winds of Spirit.

To do this is to walk toward the sun dance tree in the center of our life, and to attempt to bring the powers of the four sacred directions into balance in our hearts. And on our journey, to "always know where one's hooves will land," like Buffalo, is to realize a heightened awareness: it is to be fully present right here and right now. It is to be disciplined in freedom, as opposed to being controlled by desire and fear. It is to realize an awakened mind—a mind infused with clarity of vision and softened by the waters of the heart. It is to walk lightly on the Earth in a compassionate and caring manner. It is to embody integrity, beauty, wisdom, and compassion in the midst of a suffering world.

There is a striking resonance between the Way of Care as expressed in the Plains Indian Give-Away, and ritualized in the Sun Dance, and the Buddhist Way of the Bodhisattva. The Bodhisattva dedicates his or her life to realizing *bodhicitta,* an awakened heart, a heart of love and compassion that naturally and unconditionally cares for the welfare of others. Sakyong Mipham Rinpoche, the son of the charismatic Tibetan Buddhist teacher Chogyam Trungpa Rinpoche, describes bodhicitta in words that could have been spoken by Black Elk or any other American Indian medicine person:

> Within the bewildering maelstrom of thoughts and emotions that keep our sense of self solid, each of us already has the seeds of love and compassion. Bodhicitta is the radiant heart that is constantly and naturally, without self-consciousness, generating love and compassion for the benefit of others. It's a stream of love and compassion that connects us all, without fixation or attachment. It has a tender sadness to it, like a wound that remains eternally exposed. It's our true nature.

A great sadness of our times is that the virtues of caring and selflessness are not held up as ideals. As we pursue our own self-aggrandizing whirlwinds of desire, consumption, and blind ambition, we are running away from ourselves too fast to pay attention to our own suffering, let alone the suffering of another. We are afraid and mistrustful. Our hearts have become hardened. Our child's heart has armored itself into a false posture of protection against the pains of a world run amok. It does not have to be this way, for he winds of Spirit blowing across the Plains have never ceased. They can at any moment crack open the hardened carapace around our hearts, allowing the seeds of Care therein to spread across the land.

In sum, what Buffalo and the Give-Away show us is that life and death are one within the great cosmic circling of life. Buffalo mirrors to humans that, by selflessly sacrificing for the sake of the Other, all the people may realize a more abundant life, for Care is the sacred blanket that holds a community together and warms everyone's heart.

Wolf:

Guide to the Sacred Mountains

Of the many paths that there are in this life,
There is only one that is worthwhile—
The path of the truly human being.

— AMERICAN INDIAN PROVERB

Jumping Mouse immediately began to investigate his new surroundings. There were even more things here than in the other
places, busier things, and an abundance of seeds and other things
mice like. In his investigation of these things, suddenly he ran upon
a gray wolf who was sitting there doing absolutely nothing.

"Hello, Brother Wolf," Jumping Mouse said.

Wolf's ears came alert and his eyes shone. "Wolf?! Wolf?! Yes,
that is what I am, I am a Wolf!" But then his mind dimmed again
and it was not long before he sat quietly again, completely without
memory as to who he was. Each time Jumping Mouse reminded
him who he was, he became excited with the news, but soon would
forget again.

"Such a great being," thought Jumping Mouse, "but he has no
memory." Jumping Mouse went to the center of this new place and
was quiet. He listened for a very long time to the beating of his
heart. Then suddenly he made up his mind. He scurried back to
where Wolf sat and he spoke.

"Brother Wolf," Jumping Mouse said…

"Wolf?! wolf?!" said the wolf…

"Please listen to me. I know what will heal you. It is one of my
eyes. And I want to give it to you. You are a greater being than I. I
am only a mouse. Please take it."

When Jumping Mouse stopped speaking his eye flew out of
his head and Wolf was made whole. Tears fell down the cheeks

of Wolf, but his little brother could not see them, for now he was blind.

"You are a great brother," said Wolf, "for now I have my memory. But now you are blind. I am the guide into the Sacred Mountains. I will take you there. There is a Great Medicine Lake there. The most beautiful lake in the world. All the world is reflected there. The People, and all the beings of the Prairies and Skies."

"Please take me there," Jumping Mouse said.

Wolf guided him through the pines to the Medicine Lake. Jumping Mouse drank the water from the lake. Wolf described the beauty to him.

As Jumping Mouse investigates this new place, he discovers that it is even better for a mouse than the other places he has stopped at. Surprisingly, it seems that the farther he travels on a spiritual path the more material things are provided for him. This would seem to run counter to the logic of Western materialism, which states that an individual must engage in an endless struggle in order to attain the comforts and luxuries that make life pleasurable. On the contrary, however, the story suggests that by joining the profane and the sacred through right action (selflessness and care) all that is needed materially will be made available without a self-serving struggle.

In this new place Jumping Mouse encounters Brother Wolf, and it quickly becomes evident that Wolf has lost his memory and does not remember who he is or why he is there. He has forgotten his true nature and calling. In response to this situation Jumping Mouse retreats to "the center of this new place and was quiet." He turns inward and cultivates a quiet mind, a meditative stillness. Coming to a decision, he returns to Wolf and tells him that he knows what will heal him. "It is one of my eyes. And I want to give it to you." As soon as he stops speaking his other eye flies out of his head, and Wolf is instantly made whole. His memory is restored. He remembers that he is the guide to the Sacred Mountains and offers to take Jumping Mouse there.

Jumping Mouse's encounter with Brother Wolf is truly astonishing. In response to Wolf's loss of memory, Jumping Mouse sacrifices his other eye, leaving himself blind. This act truly defies reason. His world is now thrown into utter darkness; *he* is thrown into utter darkness, exposed and unable to defend himself against dangers.

The darkness and vulnerability that Jumping Mouse experiences at the base of the Sacred Mountains stand out as apt metaphors for our human existential situation. Although we expend a tremendous amount of energy to shield ourselves from this realization, it is precisely where we find ourselves in each moment. From a Buddhist perspective, human beings are plunged in the darkness of the ignorance of our true nature, which is understood as our inherent capacity to realize an awakened heart. This ignorance causes a gnawing dissatisfaction that under optimal conditions acts as a goad to the quest for awareness. Often, however, we try to quell this dissatisfaction by means of external remedies that never really work, such as acquiring more things, landing a higher paying job, getting a divorce, moving to a bigger house or another city. Resisting at some level the full awareness of our dissatisfaction, we live our lives unaware of our ignorance. Instead, we delude ourselves into thinking that we know who we are, that we are in control of ourselves and our world, and that satisfaction can be derived from the pursuit of material possessions and money.

The opposite, however, is the case. Far from being in control of our lives, our minds are ruled by cravings that never quite bring ultimate satisfaction, and fears that blind us to the true nature of reality. It seems that the more we get, the more we want and the more afraid we are of losing what we have, thereby setting in motion the perpetual treadmill of grasping and its attendant suffering. Moreover, our world constantly turns out to be unreliable, transient, and contingent. The pleasures we do experience are ephemeral and, try as we might to duplicate them, we can't; pain then blindsides us from out of nowhere. Control, as it turns out, is merely a convenient fiction that shields us from the awareness of the unstable, unpredictable ground we walk upon.

Plunged into utter darkness, Jumping Mouse now experiences the full impact of his vulnerability and contingency. However, having willingly placed himself in this position through an act of selfless compassion, he has created the possibility of seeing through his ignorance to an awareness of freedom. In other words, having willingly humbled himself—crouching down as low as he is able—he has unwittingly prepared the ground for his great leap into freedom.

From the perspective of the ego, to willingly give up one's eyesight is insane. However, from a spiritual perspective, to give up one's sight for the healing of the Other without any promise of reward is truly an act of great courage and compassion—an act of an undefended heart. The quest that Jumping Mouse has been on has really been a journey to the center of his own heart. And, in the end, his physical loss is really a metaphor for a symbolic death and rebirth.

Symbolically, Jumping Mouse has surrendered the last vestiges of his habitual egoic ways of perceiving and of being in the world. Our eyes are used by the ego as our first line of defense. It is primarily through sight that the world first enters our awareness, and then, based on what we observe, we immediately determine who and what are safe or dangerous, inviting the former, avoiding the latter. Without our sight, it is more difficult to make these judgments, and control is compromised.

Thus, with the loss of his sight, Jumping Mouse has symbolically wiped the slate clean of the biological and psychological elements that constitute the structure of egoic consciousness—a structure that is primarily grasping and defensive in nature. Through his selfless Give-Away, he has severed his instinctual and conditioned attachment to the illusion of a separate self, who is always trying to control his world.

At the deepest level, Jumping Mouse has severed his attachment to the attitudes, beliefs, assumptions, defenses, and values that constitute a way of perceiving in which the only things that are real are what can be seen with his own eyes—the visible, material world and all it has to offer in terms of pleasure, security, recognition, and power. Within this worldview, the invisible world of Spirit is merely a myth—a religious or romantic illusion. If we liken these structural elements of egoic consciousness to the furniture of a house, we can say that Jumping Mouse has thrown out all of the furniture in his house, rather than just rearranging it—a safer and easier option for most of us.

Through his selfless act, Jumping Mouse has undergone a radical transformation. Having shed his habitual, conditioned patterns and defenses, he now stands naked and undefended before the vast unknown of life. The small, frightened ego seeks to mold an uncertain and changing world into a manageable shape through various mechanisms of control, including the belief in the unchanging nature of its own existence, objective knowledge, technological mastery, emotional manipulation, psychological defenses, domination, and so on. These attempts at control, although ultimately illusory because there is nothing in life that can be controlled, represent the ego's way of seeking security in what it perceives to be a hostile world.

Many of these defensive patterns were formed early in childhood in response in our family situation. In a family marked by emotional, physical, or sexual abuse, children develop defensive strategies to protect themselves from what may seem to be potentially life-threatening situations. Some of these strategies may include withdrawal, self-blame, the repression of painful memories, dissociation, and the splitting off of parts of the self.

But even in a loving family, free of threat to his or her basic self-integrity, the child still must develop strategies to deal with the complexities and inevitable disappointments of relationships—the wounds of love that we all suffer to a greater or lesser degree. The ego of the child cannot be faulted for its efforts, for it is merely doing its job of trying to safely negotiate the interface between self and the world. However, these defensive stances become an impediment to a mature, healthy adulthood and to the higher potential of human consciousness.

Thus, Jumping Mouse's selfless act and his attendant sightlessness signals the surrendering of this egoic predisposition toward willfully asserting control over the world. In surrendering his own self-interest and the deeply rooted belief in a separate self, he now stands in utter darkness, with no cherished beliefs or defenses to anchor, protect, or guide him in the world. Even his entrenched identification with a fixed, solid, separate "me" has been swept away by the winds of Spirit. In Buddhist terms, he now dwells in the emptiness of "groundlessness," with nothing (*no thing*) to cling to. Free of any grasping, he is now open and present to whatever the world may send his way.

Usually, psychological change occurs in a piecemeal fashion, as we gradually see through and let go of the stories, beliefs, attitudes, and patterns that compromise our capacity to cope with the inevitable difficulties of life. Change of this nature can be painful and disorienting and sometimes experienced as a small death. But throwing out all of the furniture of our biologically, psychologically, and culturally conditioned ways of perceiving would turn our world upside down, like the Hanged Man card in a Tarot deck. It would be so altering, it could only be experienced as a kind of death.

A symbolic death of this world-shattering magnitude as a precursor to a spiritual transformation is a universal motif found in mystical literature, in medieval alchemy, in diverse expressions of shamanism from around the world, in the story of the Buddha's awakening, and in the historical and contemporary stories of spiritual awakening of countless ordinary men and women. To use one example, alchemical literature is replete with images of the body of the alchemist being beaten with clubs, buried alive, and dismembered. The ego-body, as the repository of base, material, self-centered desires and motives, is being dismembered so that it may be *re-membered* into a new spiritual configuration. The violence of these dismemberment images underscores the radicalness of the transformation needed to break the tenacious hold of the ego. It says that the hardened carapace of egoic consciousness needs to be shattered into many pieces so that something totally new may be reconstituted. In the end, it points toward a symbolic death that serves as the necessary precursor to a radical liberation, a liberation from the limitations of a separate self. Echoing a universal spiritual theme, the story says you must first enter into the darkness of the unknown if you are to reach the light on the other side. In short, you must first die if you are to be reborn.

Jumping Mouse's leap into the darkness of the West, the place of death and rebirth on the Medicine Wheel, will in the end lead him to the radiance of his full spiritual potential in the East, the place of illumination and vision. In his book on shamanism *Shaking Out the Spirits,* Bradford Keeney describes the kind of transformation Jumping Mouse has undergone:

> Enlightenment is not a light that enables you to discover, realize, encounter, develop, or actualize your ordinary self. It is turning the spotlight off of one's self. *In this new darkness, the lights of others may be seen.* In this way we see with the spiritual eyes of God. We

are able to serve others employing different vision, different hearing, different touch, different understanding, and different love. [my own italics]

With Jumping Mouse's selfless act of compassion, he has stripped away any remaining obstacles to fully embracing a spiritual consciousness that places the suffering of the Other before the ego's self-absorption. In the context of our culture, he has let go of an ultra-individualism for the sake of the Other.

From a personal perspective, I can attest to the reality to which Keeney refers. A year or so ago, I had what the contemporary spiritual teacher Adyashanti calls a "nonabiding awakening" that lasted for about two months. No single experience or event ushered in this awakening. There was no dramatic "aha!" experience or a *samadhi* experience while meditating. Of course, there may have been a number of factors that contributed to it, such as my rededication to a daily meditation practice, my enthusiasm about the way of the bodhisattva, the writing of this book, and becoming a hospice care volunteer.

But I really have no way of knowing for certain. It came out of the blue. All I knew was that somehow my usual way of seeing others and the world had been radically transformed. I no longer saw others as separate from me. Instead, I saw my face in everyone; there was no difference between us, other than the obvious ones of gender, appearance, and personality. I saw that each of us desires happiness and freedom from suffering, and as such we are brothers and sisters, and that in the midst of the difficulties of living the only way to be with each other is kind and compassionate.

Miraculously, the filter of defenses, fears, and judgments through which I normally perceived the world dissolved. The protective walls that shrank my world into a small, narrow preoccupation with my own self-interests fell away. I truly felt the oneness of all things and was filled with compassion and love for all beings. My ego no longer took center stage; as it receded into the background, a deeper experience of connection with others and an attendant joy emerged.

To some extent it was as though my past had died. Of course, I still had memories and personality traits, but I no longer lived in the prison of my personal story. My old story that I'd been carrying around inside me for decades had ceased to exist.

In my youth, this story was in the foreground and ruled my life; as a middle-aged man, it was still with me, though somewhat tempered by years of therapy and experience. But now I was no longer the son of an abusive, alcoholic father, who had lived as an outsider a good part of his adult life, who had been haunted by shame, fear, and anxiety, and who had hidden behind a wall of arrogance and anger. I felt as though the weight of my past had been lifted off my shoulders. I felt light, open, free, and loving.

This way of being was exhilarating, liberating, ecstatic. I felt more alive than I had ever felt; gone was the undercurrent of anxiety and irritability that often interfered with my appreciation of life and my relationships. Life became so beautiful and juicy as though I was really tasting it for the first time. The contrast between this way of being and the old way was so radical that I saw clearly just how limiting, constraining, and stultifying the old way was. This awakening was a death and rebirth into freedom.

Unfortunately, it lasted only about two months. Then I fell back into the tight box of my old way of being—from what Buddhists call "no self" to the royal "I." The difference between the two ways of seeing was so radical that I initially experienced this descent as very painful. I acutely felt the pain of the trance of separation and of the dream I was living. Having had a glimpse of the limitless freedom of awakening, it was painful to return to the prison of my own limited consciousness. I really felt how confining and blind egoic consciousness is; I felt like I was wearing a straitjacket.

Nevertheless, the lapse into the old way of being was not total, since the aftertaste of another way of seeing remained as a guide. Now awareness and egoic consciousness existed side by side in each moment. Awareness was able to see through the patterns of my ego—not always, of course, because the momentum of habit is so strong, but often enough to slowly bring about profound change. Also, importantly, I no longer saw awakening as some remote, impossible ideal, exemplified only by extraordinary individuals and requiring lifetimes of formal practice, as some Buddhist paths claim. The capacity to awaken lies within reach of each of us right here and now.

This view is very important, for it burns away self-doubt, skepticism, and irresoluteness, leaving instead the burning immediacy of the possible. As such, it was a blessing that inspires me as I continue on the pathless path to the spaciousness, openness, and aliveness of a nondual awareness, with a burning longing in my heart and mind, like Jumping Mouse.

To return to our narrative, it is appropriate that Wolf appears out of the West as the guide for the last leg of Jumping Mouse's journey. Wolf is the epitome of the wild spirit. His ecstatic howling at the moon has become to our civilized minds synonymous with all that is wild and free.

In some ways, perhaps, we associate with the free-roaming wolf the freedom humans lost when, 10,000 years ago, most of our species shifted away from the nomadic hunter-gatherer way of life to a settled agrarian life. Wolf's wildness reflects that part of ourselves that once experienced the unfettered freedom of our indigenous ancestors, who were at home in the wilds of primeval forests and open savannahs, and who had, over thousands of years, mastered sophisticated techniques of ecstasy through ritual, drumming, dancing, and song.

In any case, Wolf's ecstatic, communal singing to the moon reveals a primeval connection to the powers and mystery long associated with this celestial body. Across time and cultures, the human imagination has evoked the moon and its cyclical changes as a metaphor that best captures the essence of life in general, and the human way in particular, as a never-ceasing, perpetually renewed cycle of birth, death, and rebirth.

For instance, in the imaginations of our pre-Christian pagan ancestors, the moon was worshipped as the Triple Goddess, the daughter of Mother Earth, who in different cultures assumed the names of Isis, Astarte, Artemis, and Diana. Her triple aspect expresses both the three phases of a woman's life (maiden, mother, crone) and the three phases of the moon (birth, death, rebirth), as she descends into the darkness of the new moon (death), reemerges in the horned crescent moon (growth), and then waxes into her pregnant fullness (rebirth).

The eternal repetition of these three phases reveals continuity within change; it reveals transience and eternity as different aspects of the selfsame Goddess and reflects these aspects as central to the human experience. In reference to our story, the metaphor of the phases of the moon applies to the change of consciousness Jumping Mouse has undergone, as he moves from the illusion of separateness to the awakening to the oneness of all things.

The moon's essential link to the feminine is further confirmed by her connection to the waters of life, the lifeblood of Mother Earth, via the changes in the tides she brings about and by her impact on the menstrual phases of women. All of these metaphors—Moon, Birth, Death and Rebirth, Water, the Feminine—are also symbolically associated with soul.

So Wolf, as an earthly carrier of the moon's energy, reveals himself as a threshold figure whose role is that of the initiatory guide to the deepest mysteries of the soul—the mysteries of death and rebirth. As a representative of a soul, or lunar, perspective, he revels in shadows, hints, nuance, moist earthiness, shifting feelings, heart, ambiguity, paradox, ecstasy, and mystery.

In our own Western tradition, as presented in Greek mythology, these qualities are associated with the god Dionysus, who represented the cyclical, regenerative powers and mysteries of Nature. Through this connection, Wolf may be imagined as a threshold figure who, like Hermes, guides the initiate to the portals of Dionysian rapture—the entrance into an ecstatic experience of the immanence of the gods and goddesses in Nature. In his howling at the moon, Wolf expresses wild joy.

In terms of the Medicine Wheel, Wolf symbolizes the Looks-Within place of the West direction—the place of the inward turn toward soul. In responding to Wolf's loss of memory by sacrificing his eyesight, Jumping Mouse is thereby brought into the darkness of the waters of his soul life and is initiated into the secret knowledge of the cycle of life, death, and rebirth that has driven and guided the spiritual quest for millennia. Paradoxically, by traveling into the darkness and through to the other side, Jumping Mouse will discover the light of his wild, free, and holy nature. By way of rich and mysterious imagery, the story says that before Jumping Mouse can reach the heights of his Eagle spirit in the East on the Medicine Wheel, he must first descend into the depths of his Wolf soul in the West.

In the psycho-spiritual ecology of the Medicine Wheel, soul and Spirit function as counterbalances to each other. The soul plays a critical role in the spiritual journey as the fertile, receptive, moist ground within which the seed of Spirit may be planted. Furthermore, the subterranean chambers of the human soul are the repository of ancestral memory and hence carry echoes from our remotest past into the fervent longing of the present.

Thus, Wolf's loss of memory in the story points to his essential link to memory. In fact, Wolf is the Keeper of Memory, just as Frog is the Keeper of the Water. And the two—Wolf (memory) and Frog (water)—share a special kinship in the process of transformation, in that the memory of the ancient ones who have journeyed to the Sacred Mountains runs like a Great River of possibility through the soul of Wolf and each of us.

In American Indian tales, Wolf, like his brother Coyote, has been linked to the Trickster archetype. In these stories, the Trickster functions as an agent of numinous instructions through bumbling and fumbling, revealing and concealing, paradox and contradiction, seeming to be one thing when really another, playing all matter of tricks and deceptions on the unsuspecting initiate who seeks induction into the mysteries.

Among the Sioux, this role is played by the *heyoka*, a clown who during important rituals does everything backward and is the source of much laughter but also much power. For instance, at the Sun Dance I witnessed, a heyoka entered the dance grounds walking backward, carrying a bucket of water. He then drew water from this bucket with a ladle and proceeded to throw the water over the shoulders of the thirsty dancers or spill it casually at their feet. Perhaps his mockery was designed to test the endurance of the dancers even further, or to bring them back to Earth from the heights of their spiritual high.

In some ways, the American Indian Trickster is akin to the tradition of "crazy wisdom" found within Buddhism, and also The Fool card in the Tarot.

In these traditions, the Trickster or Fool archetype serves an important function for the spiritual seeker. His antics caution us not to take ourselves too seriously, which is a pitfall on any spiritual path. If we get too caught up in a spiritual materialism by clinging rigidly to our spiritual insights, concepts, and experiences, the Trickster is quick to pull the rug out from underneath us as a reminder of our humanity. He warns us that nothing is as it appears to be, that as soon as we try to pin down Spirit with a concept or a name, it slips away into the night, laughing uproariously.

If Wolf is a Trickster, one might wonder whether he has really lost his memory, or whether he is playing a trick on Jumping Mouse—a trick that will present him with the opportunity to enter into the Great Mystery. Whatever the case may be, the story does tell us that Wolf cannot exist as a guide to the Sacred Mountains without a seeker.

The elder guide needs the young seeker, as much as the seeker needs a guide. In order for Wolf to fulfill his life task, there must be seekers of the Sacred Mountains. Another way to express this reciprocal relationship between elder and youth would be to say that memory (Wolf) and longing (Mouse) interpenetrate in the dynamic of the quest, as ancestral memory provokes individual longing and individual longing evokes ancestral memory.

If Wolf has truly forgotten his life task, in the same way that Buffalo was sick and dying, it is because The People have forgotten their relationship to Spirit; they have forgotten their sacred origins and their ancestors who walked the sacred path before them.

This relationship of mutual reciprocity between the young seeker and the elder guide is a part of the web that holds the living spirit of The People together. If one part of the web is broken, then the whole collapses. If the elders are shunted aside to die in nursing homes and the young have forgotten their ancestors, then the threads of connection between the past and present are broken. When this happens, the present and the future become hollow, lacking in vitality and purpose.

It is the longing and seeking of Jumping Mouse that reawakens memory in The People of their sacred origins and allows for their renewal. In our own times, it is the cries of our youth that are attempting to awaken us from the slumbers of apathy and forgetfulness.

So Wolf guides Jumping Mouse to the Great Medicine Lake. In the Medicine Lake the whole world is reflected—all beings and all possibilities. As a mirror of the Universe, the Medicine Lake stands out as an image of what Krishamurti called "choiceless awareness," a nondual awareness unclouded by preferences and agendas. It is the all-loving, all-accepting heart center of the Universe. It is an image of the pure, unconditional awareness that lies behind appearances, thoughts, and feelings. It is Consciousness itself, as the headwaters of all life—the original creatrix, from which the Great River of Life in its infinite manifestations flows into our bodies, our lives, and our hearts. It is the ever-renewing, ever-flowing, evolutionary Universal Energy that informs all life. All beings drink from the same source waters, without discrimination. It is this river of living, creative energy that joins us all together and carries the evolutionary unfolding of the cosmos toward its fulfillment. It is the healing waters of the unitary consciousness of the heart that unites and heals all beings.

From a more narrow psychological perspective, the Great Medicine Lake is analogous to Carl Jung's concept of the collective unconscious as the universal storehouse of the archetypes and myths that have given shape and meaning to the human project across the millennia. It is the juicy source that feeds the creative imagination and urges us to create and love again and again, despite setbacks and losses.

We can imagine the Medicine Lake lying in a glacial cirque high in the Sacred Mountains—a circular body of water nestled against a sheer wall of towering rock stretching up into a limitless blue sky. This image calls to mind another image that plays a prominent role in Hindu art and worship—the phallic *lingam* as the universal masculine principle standing within a circular bowl-like *yoni* representing the universal feminine principle.

In the sevenfold *chakra* symbology of the Yogic tradition, the union of these symbols of the lingam-yoni is to be found in the heart chakra (the fourth energy center). This represents the gateway through which the energies of the three lower, more bodily oriented chakras (centers associated with rootedness in the earth, sexuality, and will) are transmuted into the three upper realms of spiritual awakening.

Thus, the healing that is taking place within Jumping Mouse can be imagined as springing from the marriage in his heart of the polarities of the body and Spirit, heart and mind, the feminine and masculine, that normally are in conflict and divide the mind against itself. In alchemy, this union of opposites is represented by the sacred marriage of the King and Queen, or the Sun and Moon.

The image of the Sacred Mountains also calls to mind another image, perhaps even more ancient. In many different traditions, mountains and hills are regarded as the matrix from which all life springs: the Great Cosmic Mother. For instance, the Sioux regard Mount Harney in the Black Hills of South Dakota as the center of the Universe. Tibetans refer to Mount Everest as Chomolungma, which means Mother Goddess of the Universe; in Nepal, Everest is known as Sagarmatha, meaning Goddess of the Sky. In pagan Britain, hills were thought of as the source of life and megalithic stones were placed there in circles to denote them as sacred, ritual ground, such as at Avebury and Stonehenge.

From these perspectives, the Sacred Mountains, like a cosmic megalith, may be seen as the sacred body of Mother Earth, and the Great Medicine Lake at her base as her womb. As the primordial womb, she is the creative source from which all life emerges into being. As the primordial source, she contains all the elements and powers of the Universe in a delicate and creative balance, an original cosmic unity.

It is precisely this sense of cosmic unity that Jumping Mouse's journey reveals to him and that the symbolism of the Medicine Wheel captures. And it is precisely this vision of cosmic unity that is so woefully absent from the patriarchal religions that dominate world consciousness today.

From this perspective, then, the transformation that is taking place at the Source Waters of Life is nothing less than the creation of a third thing out of the uniting of the opposites that frame the conflict inherent to the dualistic thinking of egoic consciousness—Masculine-Feminine, Profane-Sacred, Body-Spirit, Earth-Spirit, Heart-Mind, Good-Evil, Suffering-Joy, and so on.

That third thing, or "transcendent thing" as Jung referred to it, signifies the entrance through the heart into full spiritual awareness, an awakening to Spirit that informs and unites all of life, an awakening to the fundamental oneness of all of creation. It is the possibility of this transpersonal, mythopoeic experience of the oneness of life that stands at the very beginning of the spiritual quest, and which creates the possibility for the awakening of the heart. A heart yearning for such an experience creates the possibility of being able to respond to, to be touched by, the cries of a fragmented world.

As Jumping Mouse drinks from the waters of the lake, Wolf describes its beauty. One can only begin to imagine the wondrous poetry that issues forth from Wolf, for Wolf is also a poet of the moon. Does his poetry carry echoes of his howls at the moon on a crystalline winter night, of the intoxicating balsam fir scent of an alpine forest in the midday heat of a summer sun, of the thrill of running flat out in a primeval forest in pursuit of a deer, of rejoicing at a diamond-studded night sky, of drinking from a crystal clear mountain stream?

And, then, as Wolf shape-shifts into human form, does it carry the sparkling laughter of children as they play among the grasses of an infinite Prairie, swaying like currents of breath in the wind? Does it echo the freedom of roaming across the plains and forests and mountains and rivers and valleys without ever once seeing another person? Does it sing the sad, sweet agony of a first love, over which death casts a fleeting shadow? Does it sing the glory of a lover's hand moving across the soft mystery of another's body? Does it carry echoes of the heartbreaking losses of lover, friend, parent, or child at the hands of separation, sickness, and death? Does it capture the bright smile of a child as her mother comes into view carrying the day's burdens and joys? Does it, through some miracle, contain hints of the rich silence that passes between lovers and friends? Does it speak of death as an ally and teacher on the path?

Jumping Mouse drinks deeply from the Medicine Lake, just as he drinks in the beauty of Wolf's song. Together they heal the wounds Jumping Mouse carries with him to the lake. The waters enter every cell of his body and join him to the body of the Earth, to the body of all other beings, to the body of the Universe. The beauty of Wolf's song fills his heart with joy unspeakable and heals the wounds of separation and loneliness that have marked his days of suffering in the world.

Beauty and water are the same—without them one cannot live, cannot carry on through the cries of the world. The soul dances on the waters of beauty, on the tears of grief and joy that fill the Medicine Lake to overflowing—overflowing its shores and spilling out into the heart of the world where all beings rejoice. The Medicine Lake is the eye and heart of Mother Earth, through which she sees and feels all, and all is reflected in her. When you look into her, you see all that has been, all that is happening now, and all that will be. In her timeless stillness, she carries time and becoming and memory in an eternal present of joy unbounded.

In sum, Wolf mirrors the heart as reservoir of primordial memory, and memory and questing unite The People with the ancestors in an eternal present. Wolf mirrors that to be wild and free is to be holy, which is to be wholeheartedly and ecstatically present in each shimmering moment.

May Wolf run through your days and guide you to the Sacred Mountains where you will find your brothers and sisters waiting with open hearts.

Eagle:

Flight into Freedom

*There is a very important distinction between transformation
and change. Change implies struggling against something, but
transformation does not occur through struggle. Somehow we have
been programmed to feel (1) there is something wrong with us and
(2) we need to fix it. We feel we need to change ourselves to become
better people. We need to get rid of our ugly qualities: anger, jealousy,
addiction, and all the rest. But this is an extremely aggressive and
harmful way to think about ourselves.*

—PEMA CHODRON

*The higher I go the more I see
The more I see the less I know
The less I know the more I'm free*

—RAM DASS

"I must leave you here," said Wolf, "for I must return so that I may
guide others, but I will remain with you as long as you like."

"Thank you, my brother," said Jumping Mouse.

"But although I am frightened to be alone, I know you must go
so that you may show others the way to this place."

Jumping Mouse sat there trembling in fear. It was no use running, for he was blind, he knew an eagle would find him here. He
felt a shadow on his back and heard the sound that eagles make. He
braced himself for the shock. And the eagle hit! Jumping Mouse
went to sleep.

Then he woke up. The surprise of being alive was great, but now
he could see! Everything was blurry, but the colors were beautiful.

"I can see! I can see!" said Jumping Mouse over again and again.

A blurry shape came toward Jumping Mouse. Jumping Mouse squinted hard but the shape remained a blur.

"Hello, Brother," a voice said. "Do you want some medicine?"

"Some medicine for me?" asked Jumping Mouse.

"Yes! Yes!"

"Then crouch down as low as you can," the voice said, "and jump as high as you can."

Jumping Mouse did as he was instructed. He crouched as low as he could and jumped! The wind caught him and carried him higher.

"Do not be afraid," the voice called to him. "Hang on to the wind and trust!"

Jumping Mouse did. He closed his eyes and hung on to the wind, and it carried him higher and higher. Jumping Mouse opened his eyes and they were clear, and the higher he went the clearer they became. Jumping Mouse saw his old friend upon a lily pad on the beautiful Medicine Lake. It was Frog.

"You have a new name," called Frog. "You are Eagle!"

The story concludes with the transformation of Jumping Mouse into Eagle. This transformation of a small, earthbound creature into a magnificent winged creature is truly mind-boggling. It unsettles the mind and turns it upside down. Like a Zen koan, it defies logic and analysis, thereby freeing the mind to open upon a vast spaciousness within which the imagination can soar. And once again Frog is on hand for this transformation.

As the Keeper of the Water, Frog holds the key to healing and transformation. Symbolically, it is the fluidity of water that recommends it as an agent of transformation. Rigidity resists movement and blocks growth; it seemingly realizes its apotheosis in death, but even in death it is negated by the transmutation of matter into humus that in turn feeds life. If anything, life is ever-changing, ever-flowing, ever-shifting its shape into something else; its intrinsic nature is continuous movement and metamorphosis. Nothing ever remains the same. As Heraclitus said, "You can't step into the same river twice." Both the world and the self that seeks to grasp it are a constantly shifting phantasmagoria. To try to hold onto a fixed, solid self or a permanent, predictable world is like trying to grasp water with one hand.

Again Frog instructs Jumping Mouse to get down as low as he can and jump as high as he can. Mouse's first jump at the Great River was a dress rehearsal for this great leap. At this stage of his journey he has definitely gotten down as low as he could. By sacrificing both of his eyes for the sake of the Other, without a thought of what he might gain by it, he has truly humbled himself and experienced suffering. He has completely renounced his own self-centered desires and self-importance. In total surrender and trust, he has placed his ego on the altar of Spirit and said, "Do with me as you see fit."

His acts of selfless compassion are the touchstone of genuine humility and the necessary precursor to his transformation. Having humbled himself so low, he is now ready to take the leap of his life into the potential that has laid within him from the very beginning of his journey to the Sacred Mountains. Eagle—the thing Jumping Mouse feared the most—is the diamond that lay buried in his heart and represents the freedom to be fully awake and to live with vision.

In alchemical imagery, the shining gold of our authentic presence lies in the shadows of our awareness, along with all the other feared and rejected parts of our psyches. In the words of the writer Marianne Williamson, "Our deepest fear is not that we are inadequate. Our deepest fear is that we are powerful beyond measure. It is our light, not our darkness, that most frightens us."

In the symbolism of the Medicine Wheel, which Jumping Mouse has been turning on his quest, the spiritual path entails bringing into balance and harmony, through the clarity and compassion of our vision, the powers of the four sacred directions, each of which corresponds to one of the four elements (South/Earth, West/Water, North/Air, and East/Fire) and the four faces of the psyche (Body, Soul, Mind, and Spirit). Balance and harmony is recovered in specific moments by joining together in an ever-shifting relational dynamic all these different and seemingly contradictory aspects of our psyches to form a living wholeness.

The deepest mystery and beauty of the wholeness represented in the Medicine Wheel lies in its symbolic unification of the paradoxical interplay between change (becoming) and the stillpoint at the center of change (being). It does this by offering a template for understanding human wholeness as a relational process, based on our capacity to establish a sacred relationship with the elemental forces of Nature (turning the Medicine Wheel), and to bring them into a dynamic, creative balance within our own hearts (the stillpoint at the center of the Medicine Wheel).

The wholeness envisioned here is not a fixed, solid state or self, but rather a mutable, fluid assemblage of potentiality that responds creatively and freely—that is, unconditionally—in specific moments within a relational dynamic to a person or a situation. Such unconditioned responses emerge out of a groundlessness, unfettered by conditioned fears, desires, and expectations.

This wholeness or authentic presence awaits us in the center of our hearts, as we embrace the creative potential immanent within us. In the center, we stand like the Tree of Life, bending gracefully in the winds of Spirit. The winds are constantly shifting, pushing us in new and unexpected directions, challenging us, shedding our defenses, healing our wounds, inspiring us, fanning our creative imaginations, and opening the door of our hearts and minds to the possible. Often we fall out of balance, since we are human, but then the winds rise up again to nudge us back onto the trackless path to the Sacred Mountains and we are able to recover once again the clarity of the center. As the Navajo say, it is then that we walk the Beauty Way.

And the wholeness that is both sought on the quest—and yet already present from the very beginning—is not equivalent to perfection. It is not some fixed, external ideal, from which all the dark and unpleasant aspects of ourselves have been expunged. Rather it is more akin to what the Buddhist psychotherapist Tara Brach calls a "radical acceptance" of the manifold, changing, contingent, painful aspects of our being and of the world—a liberating self-acceptance and its accompanying world-acceptance. In the moments of such radical acceptance, self-healing and world-healing become simultaneous events. In the blazing moment that the fragmented, alienated self has a glimpse of wholeness, the world, which appeared fragmented through the lens of alienation, now appears whole and radiant.

Self-Acceptance

Such self-acceptance avoids the danger of thinking that the goal of the spiritual path is to become Christ or the Buddha, to aspire to some ideal image of perfection represented by a person who lived thousands of years ago. We are not those historical persons. We are, however, fully capable of awakening to what is real in each moment. As the Dalai Lama has suggested, there is no such thing as enlightenment *per se*, viewed as a static state to be achieved once and for all; rather, there are only enlightened responses and actions in specific moments in time to a particular person or situation.

The obstacles that impede us from an awakened heart must be transformed again and again throughout a lifetime. In each moment of our lives, we have the freedom to respond wholly from an open heart, or to continue the habitual, defensive patterns of reactivity that ensnare us in the wheel of suffering. From the perspective of an awakened mind, we have a choice regarding the matter in which we respond to an uncertain world; within the snares of ignorance, choice is an illusion, since we are driven by desires and fears beyond our control.

When we fall into the trap of attempting to measure up to some external ideal of perfection, to become someone other than who we are, we are setting ourselves up for failure and self-devaluation. Such an orientation is a trap that the ego has a tendency to fall into as it desperately seeks to conquer the ambiguous, contingent, and changing nature of reality by conceptualizing some fixed and certain ideal of perfected selfhood.

Our inevitable failures at attaining this illusion of perfection cause the ego to swing back and forth between the poles of good and bad. But this vacillation only feeds the ego's inflation as it indulges its propensity toward grandiosity at either ends of the specious continuum of good and bad. Ultimately, it betrays the ego's imprisonment within the snares of dualistic, either-or thinking—either I am God or I am worthless.

Self-acceptance, on the other hand, amounts to an acceptance of our humanness, our fallibility and finitude, while at the same time bringing the soft touch of a discriminating awareness to the habitual patterns that cause suffering. As the Buddhist teacher Pema Chodron teaches, embracing ourselves with lovingkindness and tenderness, we can silence the critical internal voice that says we are not good enough and must fix who we are. With this loving, light touch, we can then bring about the transformation of our conditioned patterns of reactivity and negativity, without aggression toward ourselves. This soft touch of seeing through these patterns gradually weakens their hold over us.

Thus, self-acceptance does not preclude transformation; rather it embraces it as intrinsic to life. Further, it is only through a radical self-acceptance that transformation is possible, for a self caught up in trying to fix something that is supposedly broken is doomed to an unceasing battle against itself. Somewhat paradoxically, the ego is invested in this battle, since it is yet another way for it to assert control through critical judgments about our progress on the path.

But a mind divided against itself cannot bring about transformation. Self-serving effort and struggle only keep the mind engaged in an endless project of self-improvement. Real transformation originates in a place deeper than the mind: it springs from the spacious openness of unconditional awareness from which thought itself rises. This natural state of awareness is our birthright—the light with which we came into the world.

Self-acceptance amounts to accepting our life as it has been lived—with its human mixture of darkness and light. It also involves taking full responsibility for our life—its failures and successes, its pain and joy—without affixing blame on someone else or the world. When we have been injured by another, we can acknowledge the injury and all of our feelings, and at the same time accept our own responsibility in the relational dynamic; or, if that is not possible because of the nature of the wound, such as in the case of childhood incest, then, at some point, we can take responsibility for the way we have chosen to live our lives in reaction to our wound.

Admittedly, this is not easy, especially given the horror of what humans do to each other; yet, when we don't take responsibility for our reactive patterns we are condemned to repeat the story of ourselves as a victim, and thereby remain blinded by our own anger, sadness, and fear. As I well know, our attachment to victimhood can be insidious: it can be difficult to ferret it out from the tangle of feelings surrounding a wound. But in order to earn the freedom of our Eagle wings, we must acknowledge the victim with tenderness; as we direct love to that wounded part of ourself, it will slowly loosen its hold on us. Here we need only recall Frog's words to Little Mouse at the Great River: "Do not let your fear and anger blind you. What did you see?" Instead of feeding the wounded victim part of ourselves, we can reach for the freedom and joy that is our birthright—the radiant mountains that lie on the horizon of our longing, the diamond hidden in the dark compost of our suffering.

Finally, another layer of acceptance involves an encounter with death. There are three layers to this acceptance, according to the structure of the Death Lodge, which is often an integral component of a Vision Quest.

First, as all of the major world religions teach, if we are to fully embrace our life, we need to accept the reality of death, since death is an inescapable part of living. An unhealthy feature of our culture is its denial of death. As a culture we are driven by a pursuit of a superficial happiness, which is itself fueled by both a compulsive demand for the instant gratification of desires and a fierce avoidance of pain and suffering—all the things that remind us of our own mortality. The dominant culture goes all out in its efforts to put a happy-face sticker over the harsh realities of sickness, aging, and death.

Second, we need to accept the reality of our own death. Each of us is going to die. You are going to die, I am going to die. No one is immune from death; it is the one thing in life of which we can be absolutely certain. Everything that we hold onto so tightly and dearly as essential to our own identity is going to come to an end some day. All will be lost—our material possessions, our house, our property, our accomplishments, our friends, our loved ones. There will be nothing of us left on this material plane. All that will remain will be our spiritual offerings: how we touched other people, how well we loved those dear to us, how we lived our life. Did we live life with grace or complain bitterly of life's disappointments? Did we love deeply or hold back? Did we accept others or judge harshly? Did we express gratitude or bemoan our fate?

Third, we need to accept the reality that the time of our death is uncertain. We could die in the next moment and not way off in the distant future, as we may like to think. This very moment could be our last. That oncoming car traveling at 50 mph could suddenly swerve directly into our path and it would be all over for us in an instant. Or, walking up the stairs to prepare for bed our heart could suddenly give out. Although our minds may tend to convert death into an abstraction that happens to other people or resides way off in a hazy future, death always hovers just beneath the radar of our awareness.

Among some shamanic traditions, death is seen as always walking behind us with his hand outstretched ready to tap our left shoulder and take us with him to the underworld. Fully taking in the immediacy of death lends an immediacy to each moment, giving it an intensity that might otherwise be lacking due to dulling routines and the stresses of daily life. Fully taking in the reality that *this* breath, *this* thought, *this* act may be my last, changes the way we see and respond to life. We see life as a priceless gift, for which the only adequate responses are appreciation and gratitude. Further, as the Buddhists remind us, we see that being born as a human being is a precious gift, since we are afforded the opportunity to awaken to our true nature; or, more accurately, pure awareness can awaken to itself through us.

By way of analogy, think of how it is when, after a long illness, we finally return to health. We are filled with gratitude and appreciation for simple pleasures that we normally take for granted. Just to get out of bed and to walk outside in the sun fills us with joy. Or, if you have ever had a close brush with death, then you know well this feeling of gratitude at being alive. In this way, the immediacy of death can be a powerful ally on the path to being fully awake, for it strips our awareness down to what is essential in each moment. The immediacy of death thrusts us into the fire of each radiant moment with an intensity of presence that liberates us from our dissatisfaction and disconnection. In such delicious moments, as Yeats wrote, "It seemed, so great my happiness/That I was blessed and could bless."

Ultimately, self-acceptance springs out of such a radical encounter with death. Acceptance allows us to fully inhabit our emotional bodies in each moment, whether pleasurable or painful, without either attachment or avoidance. If we cling to a pleasure either by living in the past or by futilely trying to hold on to it in the present, we are condemned to suffering. The past can never be recaptured, and the moment of pleasure inevitably fades away. When we try to avoid pain at all costs by chasing ephemeral pleasures, we are only compounding our suffering because we are in flight away from what is real. Likewise, if we cling in our minds to a pain or insult endured, we are trapping ourselves in the prison of victimhood and its ceaseless tale of misery and bitterness.

In its most radical realization, acceptance amounts to being ready to die in each moment. Ideally the way to die, and thus to live, is with a clean slate, such that there is not a buildup of regrets, of words unspoken, of love or forgiveness withheld, of forgiveness unasked for, of actions held in check, of risks not taken. If we could live each day of our lives as though it were the last, then we could live with greater tolerance, patience, awareness, compassion, and integrity—we could walk our talk. This, of course, is not an easy task for any of us. It requires mindfulness and a lightness of heart to accept ourselves with tenderness and lovingkindness whenever we act in a way inconsistent with our heart aspirations.

The following poem by Antonio Machado captures the interweaving of acceptance and transformation.

> *Last night, as I was sleeping,*
> *I dreamt—marvelous error!—*
> *that I had a beehive*
> *here inside my heart.*
> *And the golden bees*
> *were making white combs*
> *and sweet honey*
> *from my old failures.*

Trust

When Jumping Mouse jumps as high as he can, Frog yells to him "Hang on to the wind and trust." Once again, Jumping Mouse is being asked to surrender himself to the winds of Spirit, to trust that he will be led in the right direction and that he will be okay. In this final leap, however, he is being asked by Spirit to face his fear of death head-on. A similar leap of faith can be found in the Russian folk tale "The Firebird."

> In spite of many adventures in the service of the King's desires for this and that, a young hunter has been condemned to death at the bidding of the woman that the King wants to marry—a woman whom the hunter has brought to the King, against her will, from the Land of Never at the end of the world. The hunter is to be thrown into a boiling cauldron of water. But he has one last request which the King grants. It is to see his trusted horse one last time.
>
> Now this is no ordinary horse: it is a horse of power who possesses a secret, primal knowledge of all that is wild and free. The horse tells the young hunter that instead of letting the King's servants throw him into the cauldron he is to break free and leap into it of his own accord. The young hunter does as instructed. Twice he emerges from the boiling waters only to be sucked back down again. But then he emerges a third time and leaps from the cauldron. He stands before the King, and the King and all his subjects marvel at his beauty and the light that emanates from

him. Envious of the young hunter's beauty, the King jumps into the boiling cauldron and is killed instantly. The King is buried. And then since a great feast has been prepared for the marriage of the King and the beautiful Vasilisa and all the King's subjects have assembled for a marriage, Vasilisa celebrates the wedding feast with the hunter, and they become the rulers of the realm and long live in love and accord.

The young hunter, like Jumping Mouse, is obeying the laws of a different reality than that of the King, who is motivated solely by self-serving desire. The hunter takes a leap of faith into what could only be his certain death. Leaping into the unknown of death, he not only survives, but is transformed into the glory of his shining presence. His spiritual royalty shines from his countenance and draws the beautiful Vasilisa to him. They marry, giving concrete expression to the alchemical marriage of King and Queen that has taken place in the hunter's heart, within which the seemingly polar opposites of questing (masculine) and surrender (feminine) have been brought into balance. When the King and Queen are married, Heaven and Earth are united, and the lands are fruitful, the animals bear young, and the people live in peace and harmony.

When the dualistic separation between earthly existence and spiritual consciousness that prevails in conventional consciousness is transcended, inner and outer landscapes are reconciled and brought into harmony. Similarly, Jumping Mouse's leap of faith marries Earth and Sky, Body and Spirit, and he knows the grace and glory of freedom, which is symbolized in the flight of the Eagle.

Freedom

The flight into freedom that Jumping Mouse experiences at the shores of the Great Medicine Lake is a possibility that will probably elude Old Mouse, for he lives in a world that is based solely on material values and hence narrowly circumscribed in terms of its possibilities. His worldview prevents him from seeing beyond his fear to the spiritual ground of existence. As we've seen, Old Mouse has shielded himself from the possibility of authentic freedom within an illusory cocoon of safety and certainty. He has deluded himself into thinking that he knows what is real and what is not real, when, in fact, he only knows the limits of his own fear. His knowledge gives him a false sense of security and independence from the contingent and relational nature of reality.

This false sense of independence and freedom rests on the biggest illusion of all: the illusion of an isolated, separate self. And, as the Buddhist Stephen Batchelor says in *Buddhism Without Beliefs*, "Ironically, this alienated self-centeredness is then confused with individual freedom." Because we have the freedom to pursue our self-centered desires, we think that we are free, when in actuality we are prisoners within the narrow cells of our own conditioning and alienation.

Jumping Mouse's acts of selfless compassion, on the other hand, release him from the dictates of self-centered desire and the constraints of fear. Each jump and sacrifice that he makes releases him into the relative freedom that lies at the heart of existence. Each is an ecstatic leap into life as a continuous, dynamic process of change and relationship. Each act carries him outside himself (ecstasy) to where he finds himself in a dynamic relationship with what is Other. Freedom makes such acts possible and emerges in the act itself, which in turn opens the door to further possibilities of delight.

Of this freedom, Batchelor says,

> Reality is intrinsically free because it is changing, uncertain, contingent, and empty. It is a dynamic play of relationships. Awakening to this reveals our own intrinsic freedom, for we too are by nature a dynamic play of relationships. An authentic vision of this freedom is the ground of individual freedom and creative autonomy. This experience, however, is something we recover at specific moments in time.
>
> As long as we are locked into the assumption that self and things are unchanging, unambiguous, absolute, opaque, and solid, we will remain correspondingly confined, alienated, numbed, frustrated, and unfree.

So, as long as we believe, like Old Mouse, that reality is absolute, certain, and unchanging, and that it is these very qualities that define our freedom, we will remain trapped in the prison of an illusion and remain fundamentally unfree. In reality, the antithesis of our belief is true. It is the nature of reality as changing, uncertain, and contingent that allows for the possibility of freedom, rather than condemning us, as the logic of Old Mouse would have it, to an unknowable and hence unfree world.

It is paradoxically the unfixed, fluid, relational nature of self and things that creates the conditions for the possibility of freedom; that is, for the possibility of the full blossoming of imagination and the creative potential of the human spirit in each situation and each relationship. As we leap over the constraints of fear into the unknown that surrounds us in each moment, we are able to find our Eagle wings.

Vision

In the Medicine Wheel, Eagle represents the Medicine Power of the East, the power of awakening, of illumination, of vision. Eagle, who soars the highest in the sky of any of the winged people, is seen by American Indians as a messenger of Great Spirit. Although soaring high, Eagle always maintains a connection to the Earth, as his piercing gaze constantly searches land and water for food. In fact, Eagle's medicine comes from uniting Earth and Sky.

For humans, this is mirrored in the need to live connected to Spirit and yet at the same time never losing our connection to the body of the Earth and to our own emotional body. To gloss over the dark aspects of Mother Earth (her destructive potential, her ambiguity, her contingency, her mystery) and our own darkness (our destructive potential, our vulnerability, our uncertainties, our resistance to change) with a New Age fantasy of pure light and redemption, free of any darkness, is to live an illusion. This is a real danger on any spiritual path.

For instance, when I was in my thirties I went through an intense, semi-hermetic period of spiritual exploration that included long hours of meditation. During one meditation, I was bathed in a glowing light that seemed to enter every pore of my being. I felt a great peace. I felt that I was being embraced with a loving light. In a state of rapture, I went outside and everything around me shimmered with this extraordinarily pellucid light. I had a taste of pure bliss. After this experience, I deluded myself into thinking that I had reached a pretty high spiritual ground. In reality, however, I lacked the psychological means of integrating this experience into my everyday life. Instead of bringing me into a deeper relationship with the world, this experience separated me farther from life by feeding the spiritual arrogance of my ego. I had lost connection to my body and to real life.

This was brought home to me dramatically one day at my job as a school bus driver. As a student was getting off the bus, he informed me that another student was going to beat him up once they got off. In some inexplicable state of passivity, induced in part by meditation and a distorted sense of karma, I did nothing to intercede. Afterward, I regretted my inaction.

This, however, is not to fault meditation as a valid tool of spiritual self-discovery. As with any spiritual discipline, what is gained is dependent upon the psychological maturity of the practitioner. In my case, my spiritual practice was motivated, in part, by a need to escape an inner pain that had not been adequately addressed. Later, I entered psychotherapy and started to do the inner groundwork necessary for such spiritual experiences to really take root and bear fruit in everyday life.

A similar cautionary tale can be found within the yogic tradition. Once a seeker with Trickster qualities sought out a famous yogi, who had been meditating in a cave high in the Himalayas for many years. Upon arriving, he asked the yogi what he had learned after all these years of meditation. The yogi humbly replied that he had been practicing patience. Immediately the visitor began to disturb the few possessions the yogi had in his cave. Through it all, the yogi sat patiently. But when the visitor began to toss one of the yogi's most sacred books around the cave, the yogi erupted into a fit of rage. The visitor smiled and asked, "What about patience?"

The message is clear: it is easy to practice patience when you live in isolation in a cave of your own making; it is easy to be "spiritual" apart from the rough edges of life. To embody our vision in our everyday lives is the real challenge. Real vision comes when it is united with praxis, a practice in life, or life as practice; in other words, it emerges out of the heat and tension of relationship.

When this happens, life itself becomes our most trusted and severest teacher. For instance, it reflects back to us when our "spirituality" becomes sanctimonious, or when our intentions are not quite so free of egoism as we would like to think, or when our heart hardens toward someone who pushes our buttons or toward a loved one who has hurt us, and so on.

A similar theme of spiritual embodiment can also be found within alchemical symbolism. The seemingly chemical operations in alchemy are really metaphors for the transmutation of the "lead" of our ego-body—its darkness, fears, defenses, projections, immature desires—into the "gold" of our true nature. After a regimen of purification (the *albedo*, the whitening), during which the leaden aspects of the psyche are cleansed, the final stage is referred to as the *rubedo*, the reddening. The reddening process involves bringing blood back into the "whitened," purified psyche. In other words, it involves embodying Spirit, bringing Spirit back into the body and spiritualizing the body.

In a similar fashion, Jumping Mouse purifies and humbles his ego through self-sacrifice and surrender. Having purified his ego of its self-centeredness and arrogance, he then drinks the healing waters of the Great Medicine Lake—the waters of wholeness. As he drinks the waters, he brings Spirit into his body—uniting body and Spirit, ancient memory and present longing. Through this unification, he is transformed into Eagle. The unfathomable mystery of this transformation liberates the mind from its reliance on concepts and the known.

At dawn Eagle lifts off a high crag on the Sacred Mountains. The Great Eastern Sun illuminates the tips of its white tail feathers. Eagle dances with the sun, soaring, gliding, wheeling on solar thermals high above the green, undulating grasses of the Prairie—he epitomizes free play. The People, who have forgotten, look up and their spirits soar with memory. Into their troubled lives, Eagle carries the possibility of freedom, of illumination, of far-seeing vision, of seeing clearly with the eye of the heart. Eagle calls that there is always the possibility of seeing farther, of seeing more clearly, of including more in our vision, of awakening from the slumber of ignorance and forgetfulness. Eagle inspires The People to leap onto the Unknown. The ecstatic flight of Eagle inspires The People to reach for freedom—to embrace wholeheartedly and delightedly the changing, contingent, creative nature of ourselves and the world in each luminous moment of existence. Eagle teaches the freedom Pure Presence.

Eagle calls to us to free ourselves from the shackles of conformity, cultural conditioning, the need for approval from others, the need to be perfect, the need to realize some grandiose self-image, the tendency toward impulsive reactivity, compulsive desire, fear, the prison of victimhood, and our personal histories that condemn us to travel down familiar paths. Eagle calls to us to throw off these shackles and to soar fearlessly into the unknown, always remembering that the soaring is not possible without the departure and return point of the Earth. Jumping Mouse, as a creature of the Earth, has something invaluable to teach Eagle as well: the medicine of humility and greatness of heart.

In sum, Eagle teaches us that freedom emerges out of the fusion of grief and beauty. Eagle is born out of the ashes of a suffering endured, acknowledged, and transmuted in the fires of acceptance, passion, beauty, and awareness.

May Eagle lift your hearts out of the ashes of your suffering into the freedom and joy of an awakened heart.

More Stories from the Threshold

The following four Vision Quest stories have been culled from many similar ones; the names of the participants have been changed to protect their privacy. Each story reveals that silence and solitude in Nature brings about a profound encounter with Spirit through which healing takes place.

Ben's Vision Quest

Ben's story illustrates the negative impact that cultural stereotypes of masculinity can have on a man's life. As his story shows, he was able to break through the armor around his heart by allowing the boy within him to play. Playing freely in Nature released him from the bondage of the Old Mouse mentality and opened him up to connect with the freedom of his Eagle spirit.

Ben was a self-described workaholic who put work before family, friends, and his spiritual life. He was a powerfully built man of great energy who threw himself wholeheartedly into whatever project he was engaged in. However, he had come to the realization that the driven way he lived his life was driving away the people closest to him. At 51, he felt it was "now or never" to change course. He wanted to feel more grounded in his life, which to him meant being able to allow things to be as they were and to trust that they were that way for a reason. He wanted to silence the critical judge inside himself and to be more accepting of himself and others.

Ben felt drawn by Spirit to the Vision Quest. He longed to be more deeply rooted in his spirituality, which for the most part he had ignored. He sought a deeper connection to the Earth, to Nature. In his letter of intent, which is required of each participant, he said that "what seeks to be born in me is a joyful heart."

Ben's Vision Quest was truly magical. It was as though he had stepped back in time and returned to the spirit of his boyhood. His heart sang in exuberant celebration of being alive. The first two days he cried a lot out of sheer happiness. He couldn't believe how beautiful everything was. It seemed as though he could ask for things and they would happen. For instance, early one morning as gossamer threads of mist rose languidly off the surface of the lake, he sat looking out over the water and felt a longing to see an eagle. To his amazement he looked up and saw two bald eagles flying over the lake. His heart soared with them.

Ben had truly entered into a heightened state of awareness in which synchronicities of this sort are more likely to occur. When we are fully present in the moment to the world around us—free of worries and unburdened by the past—we become more acutely aware of the stream of communion between the natural world and the human soul that normally escapes our attention.

While on his quest Ben confronted a lifelong fear of swimming in lakes, where the dark waters could be hiding unknown dangers. After sitting on the shore naked for a long time trying to muster enough courage to enter the water, in a wild burst of energy he took off running into the lake and dived deep down. When he surfaced, he began splashing joyfully like a child. He felt such a sweet lightness and freedom. He told himself always to remember that once you get rid of the fear, there will be a lightness.

Water, like tears, cleanses and softens, and thus tempers the fire of the quester with the salve of surrender. Letting go creates the possibility for a heightened receptivity to the many faces of Spirit. Both are needed in the lifelong process of initiation—fire and water, passion and receptivity, East and West—but in balance. If the fires burn too strongly, the quester may be consumed by his or her obsessive, goal-oriented quest, like Icarus. If the waters prevail, the quester may drown in passivity and never complete any task. Although a self-described driven individual, Ben was able to surrender to the spirit of the child in him who was more interested in playing than in accomplishing anything.

Ben spent a good deal of time carving gifts for loved ones. All his love and joy poured forth into these gifts. For himself he carved a walking stick with a detachable eagle head. Beneath the eagle head, he hollowed out a place in which he hid love poems he'd written. Ben had never written a poem before in his life. He had a huge heart that he was afraid to show others out of fear of being rejected or appearing not to be a man. The poems, although still hidden beneath the eagle head, were expressions of his heart of compassion. Indeed, throughout the Vision Quest program, in the company of kindred spirits, Ben had been revealing more and more of his kindness and tenderheartedness.

One day as he sat carving beneath a large white pine, an eagle feather floated down and landed a few feet from him. He couldn't believe his eyes. He stood up and searched the tree for the eagle. In the uppermost branches he saw it just as it took flight. As he bent down to pick up the feather, he thought of the Russian folk tale "The Firebird," which I had told during preparation camp.

In the beginning of this story, whose conclusion I recounted in Chapter 3, a young hunter is riding his horse of power through the forest on a beautiful spring day. As he rides along, he is puzzled by the absence of birdsong. Then he sees a large curved feather lying on the path before him. The feather is larger than that of a swan, longer than that of an eagle. It lies shining on the path like a flame of the sun. Then the youth knows why no birds are singing: the firebird has passed this way and the flame on the path is a feather from its burning breast.

Suddenly, his horse of power speaks to him, warning him not to pick up the feather, for if he does, he will know trouble and learn the meaning of fear. The young hunter thinks the matter over. Certainly he doesn't want to learn fear, and who needs more trouble? But then if he presents such a feather to the king, the king will be pleased and will honor him. The youth picks up the feather and brings it to the king, who is mightily pleased. But the king then orders the young hunter to bring back the whole Firebird, thereby beginning a succession of trials of initiation the young hunter must undergo, which in the end help him discover his own true passion.

As Ben picked up the eagle feather, he felt he was reclaiming his own passion—his passion to be more alive and not consumed by his work, his passion to embrace his spiritual nature in all that he did and not to let petty concerns and fears rule his life, his passion to reveal more of his heart to the world. Eagle had transferred its energy and vision to him. He felt renewed and eager to return to his life.

When Ben returned to base camp, his face was shining with a youthful joy. His heart and soul were dancing and overflowing with love, which he showered on everyone in the group. Through Eagle, the beauty and power of Spirit had truly entered his heart. He had found the joyful heart he had been seeking on his quest. It had been present all along before he had even begun his quest, but was hidden beneath his conformity to artificial, cultural stereotypes of manhood.

Jen's Vision Quest Story

Jen's story is about making sense of her suffering, and then using the lessons learned to come into a mature expression of her adulthood. Her story illustrates the spirit of the Give-Away taking flight within her.

Jen was the first to sign up for this Vision Quest. She was very eager and determined … and scared. Doing something like a Vision Quest was a stretch for her, but she was determined to change her life.

Jen's story was filled with pain: she had suffered many disappointments and betrayals. She grew up in a rural setting. In many ways it was an idyllic life, surrounded by meadows, streams, and woods, but there were shadows cast on this pastoral scene.

Her father was an alcoholic, and her mother was emotionally abusive toward her. She was closest to her father, but his alcoholism was unpredictable and introduced chaos into her life.

At 16, Jen became an alcoholic herself and remained one until she was 33. She tended to gravitate toward abusive men and led a wild life of drunkenness and promiscuity. She married early to get out of her dysfunctional family, but the marriage ended in divorce a few years later after her daughter was born. When her daughter was two, Jen made a suicide attempt. When she was discovered and revived, she started screaming hysterically, "Where's my daughter?" This was the wake-up call she needed. She stopped drinking, began attending Alcoholics Anonymous meetings, and went into counseling.

Jen was 55 at the time of her quest. She, had been in and out of counseling for 20 years or more but still felt stuck in her life. In her words, "I am stuck and except for being sober and maybe a little wiser I don't feel I've made much headway toward my goals and my dreams." She felt that somehow she always sabotaged herself just when things started to get better in her life. As she put it, "I know that I do it, because I cannot face my own blank page."

She wanted to be a writer, but she was terrified of taking that risk. It was easier for her to stay stuck in the familiarity of her unfulfilled life, than to risk venturing forth into the unknown. In her letter of intent, she stated the following:

> I don't come to the Vision Quest to find my purpose because I
> believe I have already been enlightened to that. I come to find the
> path to use what God has given me in a healthy, helpful way. I need
> to face the fears that keep me stuck, that keep me from writing,
> from publishing my book, that keep me hiding behind twenty extra
> pounds and in work that is unfulfilling, and in unhealthy relation-
> ships that only prove what I believe to be true: that I am unlovable,
> that I am inherently flawed. Something inside wants so desperately
> to come out.

Undermining Jen was a pattern in which any time her creative energies started flowing she would undercut it and then use her ensuing paralysis as confirmation that she would never live her dreams. Her low self-worth and corresponding fear conspired against her to keep her trapped in the role of victim. Repeatedly in preparation camp, she said, "I just don't know what it is that keeps me stuck."

Her words revealed the paradox that lay at the heart of her suffering. There was a part of her that did know that it was her identification with the persona of the victim that blocked her from moving forward in her life; yet another part of her was in denial about how strong this identification was. Sometimes our ego becomes too strongly identified with our own suffering. The trade-off is that our suffering gives us a sense of specialness and prevents us from really taking the risk to go for our dreams.

Jen did a tremendous amount of inner work in preparation camp. Her honesty and tears set the tone for the rest of the group. She was on a heroic journey and was determined to unlock the mystery of her suffering. The night before the solo, as we sat around the fire, she revealed a dark stain from her past that she had never told anyone. As she sobbed uncontrollably, the group responded with total acceptance and love. In that moment, Jen had unburdened herself of a weight on her heart that had imprisoned her for years.

The conditions were now set for the Vision Quest to work a miracle. When I asked her intention for the quest, she said, "To be open to how I can use all my experiences to help humanity." When I asked what I could pray for her, she said, "Pray that as the blocks come up for me that I have the strength to get through them and to stay open to the messages."

On the first day of her quest, Jen put her tarp up and then took it down because it wasn't quite right. She did this a number of times before she realized that she was afraid of not being busy. Putting her tarp aside for the time being, she sat on a rock and sang, wrote, and played a tin whistle. It soothed her soul and stilled her restlessness.

A dragonfly, the spinner of illusion and magic, became her constant companion. She recalled a story about how the dragonfly became what he was. Dragonfly was once a powerful dragon, who was constantly puffing himself up and blowing fire to make people see how important he was. As a consequence, the Creator turned him into something small in order to teach him humility.

Jen realized that she was constantly trying to convince others how good and right she was, that she was always seeking the approval of others, rather than just being who she was. Then she saw how she was using the burdens of her past to puff herself up and to stay stuck.

At this point she stood up and announced to the world "I am not a victim!" She saw clearly that her ego used self-righteousness to reinforce the victim persona, and that both were based on fear. She then performed a ritual. She wrote on a rock the things she wanted to unburden herself of, such as anger, and threw it in the lake. Next she wrote on rocks the names of the people she loved and the things she valued. Then she threw them in the "River of Life" and made a commitment to always value them and to live her life based on them.

Another day she wrote in her journal, "Jen, look at the rich texture that is you, share your pain and experience so that others may be free of theirs. Your pain has made you compassionate—teach others. Use this gift wisely and then let it go." Jen was truly making peace with her past and this freed her to be drawn by Spirit into a fuller, more complete expression of herself. In her freedom she was able to embrace the spirit of compassion and the Give-Away.

Jen began making bead necklaces for the other questers. This Give-Away became a meditation during which each of the questers spoke to her. Sally told her that she needed to rejoice in the gifts that her mother had given her. Mary, who looked like a person in her life who was angry at her and whom she did not like, taught her that each person loves and is loved, suffers and experiences joy, and that our commonality unites us in one circle. Eli showed her the passion she had when she was 22, and that that passion was still inside her wanting to emerge. Susan, who had also been promiscuous and alcoholic as a young adult, told her to mourn the guilt she carried for her behavior, but to let go of the guilt itself. Susan said, "We've cried enough tears; it is now time to reclaim our own right to live a full and rich life."

Jen was shining when she came off the solo. She described it as the greatest experience of her life. She was exultant. Her story was so amazing. Heroically, she traveled into the darkness of her past and transmuted her suffering into the passionate, creative, giving person that she was. She had traveled full circle: the end had been within her from the beginning.

About two years after her quest I asked Jen in what ways, if any, had the experience of being alone in Nature on a quest changed her life. This is her response:

> Being alone in nature during the solo was the single most powerful experience of my life (except, I must insert, the birth of my daughter).
>
> It was not just important to the transition; it was its cause. I did not feel alone in the universe, I felt connected. I never felt fear; I felt empowered. I never felt rejected, only acceptance. I felt unrestrained; nature has no boundaries and neither did I. As I lounged in nature's womb I opened to its wisdom and became acquainted with the person I was meant to be in all her strength and glory. I was not the person I thought I needed to be in order to be accepted, tolerated, approved. I was free to be who I wanted to believe myself to be, quite possibly for the first time in my life. And I knew in those moments that all the boundaries, restrictions, judgments, and burdens were born of the enemies within, not the enemies without.

Sue's Vision Quest Story

Sue's story was a heroic journey into the darkness of her past. In her descent into the underworld, she was aided by dreams and the sacred feminine—both messengers of the soul.

At 56, Sue was due to retire in a few months from her job as a nurse. She decided to go on a Vision Quest in order to envision her life ahead without the work she knew so well. Nature had always been a source of peace and joy to her, but over the years she had been spending less and less time in the natural world because of physical problems. So her intention was to renew her connection with the natural world.

The nature of Sue's physical problems were so daunting that I seriously questioned her capacity to deal with the challenges of a Vision Quest. To begin with she was extremely allergic to the sun and strong heat. She was also allergic to a host of other things, including mold, weeds, and even trees. Her doctor had recommended that she stay indoors as much as possible with an air purifier going all the time. I was completely amazed that given these physical challenges she would even consider going on a Vision Quest, where she would have to hike three miles to base camp in the hot August sun, remain outside with minimal shelter for four days and nights of fasting, and then hike back out. I thought, "Here is a brave and determined woman."

After I expressed my concerns that her low tolerance to the sun and heat could seriously compromise her capacity to cope with the quest and perhaps jeopardize the entire trip, she assured me that if she could go at her own pace and had access to water she would be okay. Since the first leg of our hike to base camp followed a stream and after that we would be near a lake surrounded by trees, I decided to risk it and let her go out.

On the day we were to depart, I was loading each person's backpack onto my truck when I discovered that Sue's pack must have weighed close to 70 lbs! Normally a pack weighs between 35 and 40 lbs. There was no way that I could let her carry that much weight, so we went through the contents of her pack item by item, eliminating everything that was not essential.

The hike to base camp was slow going, but Sue made it. Sue also stayed out the entire four days and nights. After fasting, the hike out was much more difficult for her, but with the help of other participants, who lightened her load, she made it. Everyone was jubilant when Sue emerged from the woods and made her way to a car with the air-conditioner blasting away. This group had really come together as a tight-knit community, with everyone helping out to see that each person made it.

Sue's life story, which she spoke of before the solo, and her Vision Quest story touched each of us to the core. She had suffered a very painful past. As a child she had been sexually abused by a neighbor. Feeling that her mother had not protected her, she was very angry at her, even now after she had been dead for a few years. Before she went out on her quest she asked me to pray that she could stay focused and not drift off into painful memories.

But the nature of the quest is such that whatever needs to be looked at or healed will more than likely present itself to the quester. When the belly is empty and routines and distractions have been removed, the psyche tends to get churned up and to throw up to the surface unresolved emotional issues. And, in fact, this is what happened on Sue's quest.

The first thing Sue did when she arrived at her Vision Quest site was to build a circle of stones and wood around her site. Around the perimeter of the circle there were many "ancient ones"—moss, ferns, salamanders, and loons out on the lake. She felt safe within her protective circle and vowed never to leave it during her quest.

The protective circle as a means for women to ward off danger is a familiar theme in folk tales. For instance, in the amazing story "The Handless Maiden," a down-and-out miller makes an ill-advised bargain with the devil. One day as the miller gathered wood in the forest, an old man appeared from behind a tree and promised him great riches if he'd give him what was behind his mill. Thinking that the only thing behind his mill was a flowering apple tree, the miller agreed to the bargain. The old man said that in three years he would come to take what was his. Little did the miller know that at the time his only daughter was behind the mill sweeping the yard with a willow broom. The first time the devil came to fetch the girl he found her dressed in white and standing in a circle of chalk she'd drawn around herself. When the devil reached out to grab her, an unseen force threw him across the yard. He then left in disgust.

Sue's circle of power not only served to keep "large animals" out but also gave her the safety and strength to face an old wound. She had created a sacred circle on the body of Mother Earth, and within that larger embrace she found the courage to grieve the loss of her mother and to forgive her for not protecting her many years ago. Once again she was able to draw nurture and peace in the bosom of Nature.

While questing, Sue had two dreams that offered her guidance and support. In the first dream, a truck dumped a load of junk in her house. From this image Sue saw that she had too much clutter in her life and that she was using it to distract herself from the pain she carried inside. She saw the importance of simplifying her life and vowed to clear out the clutter from her home, just as we had done with her overloaded backpack.

The second dream presented a stark and frightening image, which was cloaked in mystery. Someone had cut down the magnolia tree in her backyard. This tree was her "sanctuary" and now it was gone. Sue was understandably shaken by this dream image. But what could the symbolic significance of this loss of her sanctuary be?

As we worked with this image, Sue began to wonder if perhaps her outer sanctuary had shielded her from her pain and her fear of the world, just as the clutter inside her house had. Perhaps, now that she had let her grief regarding her mother's death and her sexual abuse well up to the surface, she no longer needed the outer sanctuary because she was creating an inner sanctuary of healing. In addition, her reconnection with the natural world had expanded her sanctuary from the closed garden of her backyard to the open expanse of a vibrant, wild Nature. It now seemed that a sheltered existence was no longer necessary for Sue. She was being called into a more abundant life.

Sue ended her Vision Quest story by saying, "I'm happy: I have reconnected with the world of Nature that is all around me, and *I can go out into Nature.* My spirit has returned to the wilderness around me." Returning to the body of the Earth, Sue's body and spirit had been renewed after years of being suppressed beneath a cloak of pain and fear. She had returned home to her true nature—the spirit within her that could not be destroyed by the abuse she had suffered—by means of returning to her original home in Nature.

Linda's Vision Quest Story

Linda was 29. Her story is also about drawing nearer to her true nature, which contained the seeds of her potential to be a healer. This potential still lay dormant within her; however, her story reveals how Spirit may be guiding her toward its development.

Like many healers' life stories, Linda's is one of experiencing a deep wound early on. As a child she was the victim of sexual abuse. A violation of one's integrity of this magnitude is a searing wound to the psyche of a young child. The innocence and trust that are the hallmarks of a happy, carefree childhood were shattered by this violent betrayal.

To protect herself, Linda built a wall around her true nature and created a persona that was highly skilled at reading others and adapting chameleonlike to what they wanted her to be: the good daughter, the romantic partner, the self-effacing friend, the obedient employee. She became so good at putting on masks she forgot who she really was, if indeed she ever knew. She went through life believing that she had to earn the right to exist, that she had to justify her existence, rather than seeing her life as a gift with no strings attached.

A few years before the Vision Quest, Linda found what she called her "teacher." Working with this woman, Linda was able to learn about being in her body, living more fully in the moment, and being who and what she truly was. As she put it in her letter of intent, "I have begun to feel like I am finally growing into my life, my Self."

Her intention for the quest was "to shed this childhood skin …and to discover my authentic Self and to become clear about my purpose in this existence."

She had a desire to be of service to others and the planet, but she wasn't sure what form it would take. She closed her letter with the words: "My intention is to complete my transition into adulthood." Her successful passage into her fullness as a woman was impeded by the wounds of her childhood. Her initiation into adulthood would involve coming to terms with those wounds and embracing her true spirit.

Working with Linda during the four days of preparation camp was a delight. She took to the exercises of attunement to the natural world like a duck to water. It would be fair to say that she reveled in them; her spirit came alive and sparkled. Her connection with Nature was natural and profound. This was the first indication to me that she was a woman who could potentially use her medicine power for healing others.

When Linda went out to find her questing site, she was led to the site by the call of an eagle. She heard the call and took off crashing through the bushes and brambles until she got to the lake where she could see the eagle high above the water. When she stopped to look around at where she had landed, she decided to make it her home for the next four days and nights. That evening around the fire, she bubbled with enthusiasm as she told how Eagle had guided her to her site.

On the Vision Quest, Linda devoted each day to a different direction on the Medicine Wheel. She began in the South and allowed her child to do whatever she wanted to do. She let her play in freedom on the welcoming and loving body of Mother Earth, let her play in a way that she was unable to play as a child because of the ever-present threat to her own physical body. Her body rejoiced, and she experienced a tremendous liberation of her spirit.

On the second day, Linda experienced painful indigestion from acid buildup in her stomach. She drank water but that didn't seem to help. While sitting naked on a rock that jutted out into the water she saw Eagle again. She stood on her rock and cried to him. He answered her calls and circled over her three times. Then he spiraled up and up and up. Linda felt like she was rising up with him, that he was pulling her up higher. She felt an ecstatic expansion of her being.

Later as she lay beneath her tarp she heard a voice ask, "Should we tell her?" Then the voice said, "Yes, I think it's a good time now." She looked around and realized to her utter amazement that "her birch tree" had spoken. She asked the tree, which was split into seven trunks, if it had spoken. The tree said, "We did." Linda named the tree "We" and entered into a dialogue with it.

After telling the tree about her intention for the quest and about Eagle, she asked, "What can you tell me about my authentic Self?" "We" reminded her of how she was as a child. It reminded her of the openness she had felt in the presence of Nature and of her sensitivity. "We" said that her sensitivity, for which she had always been shamed, was instead her greatest gift; it allowed her to be in touch with subtle energies. In the presence of "We," Linda reclaimed that gift.

Then Linda and "We" talked about how in her heart there was so much light but she was afraid to let it shine, because in her childhood she had received many messages that she shouldn't shine too brightly. Others were jealous of her and felt threatened by her and tried to put her down. "We" told her that she needed to release her need to please others. Then "We" asked what she thought her shadow side was. Linda didn't know. Not long after that her stomach became very acidic and she threw up bile.

On the third day, dedicated to the North, Linda thought a lot about the ways she could be of service in the world. She knew it had to do with helping people find their gifts, but first she had to find her own unique gifts. She decided to do a Death Lodge ceremony that night. She laid down in a depression in the ground and said what she needed to say to all the people in her life as a final good-bye. After many tears, she rose up and began to dance. In her words, "I danced for Eagle and I cried out to Loon when he called. I danced for Mother Earth and Father Sky. I danced for the Moon and for Mars, which was leading the Moon across the sky. I danced for my life and for Mitakuye Oyasin [all my relations in Lakota] …I danced so Death might see how much I wanted to live again."

On the morning of the fourth day, the day devoted to the East, Linda came back to base camp because she continued to vomit. I gave her some Tummy Mint tea and offered her bread, which she refused. When I asked her if she wanted to go back out, she looked at me as if I had two heads. She said, "Oh yeah!" So she went back out.

Later in the afternoon she heard a small splash and then a larger splash. When she looked out onto the lake, she saw an eagle, which had just caught and then dropped a fish. The eagle was "immense" and just 25 feet from her. "My heart thudded and I cried out to him and told him that I would remember." As the last night approached she talked some more with her tree. "We" said that with regard to her gifts she just needed to keep doing what she was doing—healing herself—and that things will be revealed gradually as her life unfolds.

When Linda told her Vision Quest story, I reflected back to her how significant it was that Eagle had led her to her site and that he had played such a prominent role in her story. Eagle was constantly reminding her of her connection with Spirit and calling her forward into a life more devoted to the spirit within her and the spirit in all things. The joy that she felt in the arms of Mother Earth attested to her unique and powerful connection to the forces of Nature and that she could now use that relationship to heal herself and others. I also reflected back that it seemed that the pain in her stomach was sending a strong message that she could not avoid. Her stomach was filling up with bile secreted by the liver, which in Chinese medicine is linked to anger. So perhaps her shadow side has to do with repressed anger regarding the abuse she had suffered as a child. Linda knew this was true but was afraid, like many women, to acknowledge and express her anger.

A few months after the quest I received a letter from Linda. She had moved to a small, beautiful farm and was enjoying the quiet peace of living closer to Nature. She thought that she had been "plunked down in this quiet piece of nature so that I may learn." She was giving herself time for her gifts to ripen inside. She was examining without judgment her desire to make a difference in the world and trying to see if that was related to her old wound of having to justify her existence with some great act. For the time being she was learning to be more fully present in each moment and not worrying about what contribution she would make to the healing of the planet.

From Linda's commitment to healing, her purpose will gradually emerge. As her gift ripens inside her, it will spring from Spirit moving through her and out into the world, and not from an egocentric desire to do something great. In embryonic form, she has a natural capacity for leadership and for healing. She is a woman of Medicine Power.

* * *

There are many more stories of homecoming like these. Solitude, silence, and fasting in Nature open doors within us that have been closed for various reasons. Each door opening is also a door closing on an old storyline from the past that no longer serves us. Each opening allows more of who and what we truly are to emerge from the dark into the light.

PART THREE

Incorporation:

Walking the Pathless Path
Between Worlds

At a time when the all-embracing certainties of closed societies and belief systems no longer convince or reassure us, more and more do we find ourselves in that perplexing middle ground between communities and ideas. Having embraced this homelessness, we are at liberty to weave our way between Buddhism and monotheism, the religious and the secular, science and art, literature and myth. In exploring the fertile spaces between traditions, we open up a path that may be rooted in a specific tradition but has branched out into the no-man's-land between them all.

—STEPHEN BATCHELOR,

LIVING WITH THE DEVIL: A MEDITATION ON GOOD AND EVIL

A Culture at
the Threshold

What is—or what is to be—the new mythology? It is—and will forev-
er be, as long as our human race exists—the old, everlasting, perennial
mythology, in its "subjective sense," poetically renewed in terms neither
of a remembered past nor of a projected future, but of now: addressed,
that is to say, not to the flattery of "peoples," but to the waking of
individuals in the knowledge of themselves, not simply as egos fighting
for a place on the surface of this beautiful planet, but equally as centers
of Mind at Large—each in his own way at one with all, and with no
horizons.

—*JOSEPH CAMPBELL*

The god
Is near, and hard to grasp.
But where there is danger,
A rescuing element grows as well.

—*FRIEDRICK HOLDERLIN*

Our culture finds itself poised at a threshold where we are being called to make a momentous decision upon which the fate of our species and the Earth hangs. As David Korten claims in *The Great Turning*, before us, right here and now, stands the possibility of bringing about a Great Turning from Empire to Earth Community.

Empire represents the principles and values of the conqueror consciousness that has prevailed throughout the world for the last 5,000 years, and which has brought humanity to the brink of ecological and social collapse. In today's world, Empire is based on the principle of corporate domination, as international corporations, sup- ported by government and secured by the military, seek to exploit and control people and Nature for the sake of securing and augmenting their power and wealth.

Our dominant culture embraces the values of Empire, which manifest in economic terms in unsustainable, unlimited industrial growth at all costs, as the engines of corporate commerce seek to expand their markets into every corner of the world. The values of Empire promote materialism, greed, unlimited consumption, inequality, hatred, violence, the unsustainable exploitation of the natural world, and an ultra-individualism at the expense of the welfare of others. Old Mouse is a representative of the values of Empire, in our story and in ourselves.

Earth Community, on the other hand, represents the principles and values of a spiritual consciousness. As the name implies, Earth Community is based on the principle of partnership in relation to people and the natural world. It honors and fosters relationships of mutual reciprocity and respect among all beings—human and nonhuman—that are grounded in equality, caring, cooperation, and sustainability. In Earth Community, the rights of the individual to pursue life, liberty, and happiness yield to the well-being of the whole community of life. Like Buffalo in our story, the people of Earth Community seek to walk in balance and harmony on a sacred Earth. Like Jumping Mouse, they are motivated by Communion and Care.

Our saving grace lies in awakening from the nightmare of Empire and dreaming Earth Community into being as the living foundation of the world. At its core, this dreaming would bring about an evolution from a conqueror consciousness to a spiritual consciousness, beyond the limitations of convention and religion. It would amount to a spiritual awakening in which humanity awakens to the interconnectedness and Sacred Oneness of all beings.

Humanity is ripe for this awakening. The dangers of Empire—the chaos and suffering it has created throughout the world—have become glaringly transparent. A "rescuing element" is emerging to meet the danger.

A State of Emergence

As we stand upon this threshold, many of us can no longer make our way through the world either driven by the secular myth of the independent, ambition-consumed individual (the conquering hero) or with the consoling support of an established religious tradition. Thus, many of us live without a coherent vision that can provide us with understanding, guidance, and a moral compass as we encounter the complexities and ambiguities of these difficult times.

As a consequence, we find ourselves alone at this threshold without solid ground to stand upon. This can be a painful and challenging place to be, although at the same time exciting. How can we abide in the challenge of this "groundlessness," faced with uncertainty and the withering away of the traditional myths?

As we have seen in the elaboration of the archetypal dynamics of rites of passage in Chapter 2, an encounter with death can also be a precursor to a spiritual transformation. In other words, this groundless threshold space—this dying place—can also be a birthing place. In order for the new to be born, something has to die.

Faced with this groundlessness, we can turn to the story of Jumping Mouse for guidance.

Jumping Mouse was in a similar place of groundlessness as he stood in darkness on the shores of the Great Medicine Lake. Frog, the skillful guide between worlds, instructs him to get down as low as he can and then jump as high as he can. His guidance is to surrender in humility and then leap into the void. Like a Zen master, Frog pushes him to the edge of his fear, which is the only place that he can find the courage and freedom that has always dwelled in his heart. After Jumping Mouse has leapt, Frog says to him, "Don't be afraid. Hang on to the wind and trust!" Powerful and scary counsel. How can we take this counsel to heart?

In the emptiness of not-knowing and the agony of the dying going on all around us (both literally and symbolically), we can draw on the powers of the South direction on the Medicine Wheel. The South is the doorway to trust and innocence. We are being challenged to trust in Spirit that a way through this period of disintegration can be found, that a new way of being on Earth can emerge. When the choice is between the disintegrating forces of Empire and the hope of Earth Community, it seems clear that we are being called to take the leap by aligning ourselves wholeheartedly with the emergent vision of Earth Community.

Admittedly, this isn't an easy thing to do in the face of the chaos and violence raging in the world and in our own hearts. Moreover, as the institutions and structures that support Empire are challenged, their resistance to change will become more deeply entrenched. This entrenchment will no doubt usher in an increase in chaos and violence.

Here I'm reminded of a verse in the poem "The Invitation" by Oriah Mountain Dreamer:

> *I want to know if you can get up*
> *after a night of grief and despair*
> *weary and bruised to the bone*
> *and do what needs to be done*
> *to feed the children.*

The children always need to be fed right here and now. They need to be held and loved. They need to be fed the soul food of the new vision of Earth Community if they are to grow up healthy and sane. And we are the only ones who can feed them. As the

Hopi prophecy says, we are the ones we've been waiting for. We are the only ones who can bring about Earth Community.

Somehow in the midst of a world reeling under the burden of its imbalances, a new vision is already emerging through the constellation of multiple factors and streams of influence. Some of these influences include the wisdom of indigenous cultures, deep ecology, ecopsychology, ecovillages and intentional communities, environmental organizations, social justice groups, native rights groups, the new sciences, and the Universe Story, which celebrates the wonder and mystery of the evolutionary "cosmogenesis" of life on this planet. Each of these is a piece in a mosaic of the emerging vision.

It is important to point out that even though the traditional religious myths lack the authority they once had, there are still elementary ideas within them that are inherent within the human psyche and that can be retained in the new configuration. These ideas form the basis for the "perennial mythology" that has been passed down through the ages in a multitude of forms, yet still containing the one essential seed idea of the value of the spiritual journey inward toward awakening. Today there are many people within these established religious traditions who are embracing the values of Earth Community. They are adding their piece to the mosaic.

Somehow we must situate ourselves within the labors of this birthing process with the trust and innocence of the child, or, as is said in the Zen tradition, with a "beginner's mind"—a curious, open mind, unencumbered by concepts, beliefs, and expectations.

That, after all, is precisely what Jumping Mouse did as he ventured forth into the unknown, following the urgings of his heart. It is this heart of openness that will be the birthing ground of the new, as it creates the spaciousness to be fully present in each moment, holding in a delicate balance the energies from below and the energies from above—body and mind, matter and Spirit, Earth and Heaven.

As these energies are married in the heart, the heart overflows and expands beyond the limited horizons of the parochial, patriarchal, traditional mythologies that no longer inspire the modern imagination. This is to say that an essential element within the new orientation, which has already found a home in the modern psyche, is that it will not be limited to one absolute truth as claimed by the traditional religious systems.

Such a transcendent absolutism has only succeeded in dividing the world into separate warring camps and in separating the individual from the divine. In all likelihood, the emergent vision will not be one vision at all; rather, it will embrace a diversity of visions. Perhaps a central feature of this new orientation will be for each individual to learn how to abide in peace and awareness in the midst of uncertainty and groundlessness, without a fixed belief system. This leap into the unknown in each moment will awaken us to the reality of Pure Presence—an openhearted welcoming to what is. Within such a welcoming Earth Community will thrive.

The Recovering of the Sacred Feminine

As we stand on the threshold between worldviews, perhaps we can find guidance in a metaphor that emerged at the threshold between the Middle Ages and the modern era. In *The Legend of the Holy Grail*, the quest of the Knights of the Round Table was for the Holy Grail.

Symbolically, an outstanding feature of the Holy Grail, a chalice, is its emptiness. As an open vessel, it can hold the longings of all who may seek out the source of Spirit, in whatever form it may manifest. In this regard, it bears some resemblance to the Great Medicine Lake as a mirror of the whole world, and of the infinite possibilities of life and the human imagination.

In its emptiness, the Grail connotes the purity, beauty, and power of receptivity as an essential element in the realization of awakening. This receptivity is equivalent to surrender—a surrender that is not a passive resignation but rather an unconditional openness to the truth of the moment. In the dynamic of the quest, surrender stands as a necessary counterpoise to the immense effort needed to undertake the quest.

For the Hero to awaken from the slumber of ignorance of his true nature, he must embody a balance between effort and surrender, between the masculine and the feminine. His fiery zeal must be tempered by the softening influence of the waters of the heart. As he finds his balance, he will find himself in the natural state of awareness that has always dwelled inside him. Spirit as pure awareness will make itself known through him.

In a similar vein, when we look at our cultural distortion of the hero myth into a conqueror consciousness directed against the outer world, we can see the need for the tempering influence of the feminine. In Celtic mythology, we find support for this. When Cuchulain and his warriors returned from war, berserk with the frenzy of battle, the women went out to meet them before they reached their community and took them into their arms and lay with them. The fires of battle needed to be tempered by the waters of love and connection before the men could reenter community life. Applied to today's world, the excesses of an ultra-individualism and conquest need the waters of compassion and care in order to awaken a sense of Earth Community.

At the turning point into modernity, the Holy Grail, as a symbol of receptivity, represents the reemergence of the Sacred Feminine into a more prominent place within human consciousness after having been forced underground for centuries by the violent suppression of the Church. In other words, it represents the recovery of the feminine orientation of receptivity and openness.

In the *Legend of the Holy Grail*, this recovery is needed in order to heal the wound of the Grail King. The Grail King is the custodian of the Holy Grail, but he is unable to drink from the chalice. Symbolically, he suffers because he has lost a connection to his soul. With the drying up of the waters or the lifeblood of his soul, his life and kingdom have become a barren wasteland. It is this wasteland condition that sparks the quest to restore soul to the world, to bring the waters of life back to an arid Earth, awakening seeds hidden in the dark. And, according to the legend, it was Parsifal— the Innocent Fool—who finally asked the question that healed the Grail King. That question was, Whom does the Grail serve? From a Christian perspective, the Holy Grail serves the soul of the world by bringing the spirit (lifeblood) of Christ back into the world. From a modern perspective, the Holy Grail serves the soul of the world by creating a heart opening to receive the animating spark of Spirit.

Today, like the Grail King, we suffer from a similar wound of disconnection from the vital waters of the soul and the *anima mundi* (the soul of the world), and our world is fast becoming a wasteland. But the healing powers intrinsic to the image of the Holy Grail point to key elements within the dynamics of the quest that may offer guidance to us as we initiate our own quests.

As the goal of the quest, the Holy Grail functions symbolically to turn the gaze of the seeker inward toward the open well of his or her own soul, whose seat is the heart. In other words, the openness of the heart holds the key to the possibility of reconnecting with the vital waters of life and of reembracing life in all of its magnificent diversity and beauty. Within the heart lies the potential to embrace all of creation without discrimination as a sacred landscape. Within the heart lies the possibility of embodying Pure Presence and compassion before the mystery of an unfolding Universe.

The awakened heart is touched by a sense of the Spirit that dwells within all things, by a sense of Oneness in the many. The receptivity, openness, and inclusiveness of an awakened heart defies the parochial, monotheistic, and exclusionary patriarchal attitudes toward the holy that have contributed to the spiritual wasteland and wars of the modern world. The awakened heart can be seen in the generosity and compassion of the American Indian Give-Away and the Buddhist Bodhisattva. It is precisely its emptiness that allows it to hold the whole world in its loving embrace without discrimination and to overflow with love and compassion back into a troubled world.

This open heart also is the wellspring of the creative imagination, which continually reminds us of the mystery and beauty of creation, of our interrelationship with all beings, and of our Oneness in Spirit. It reminds us that, despite our many differences, each of us, human and nonhuman, is in the same boat on the waters of life; each of us desires happiness and freedom from suffering.

Just as the quest traverses the pathless terrain of the heart, it is also undertaken without a definitive horizon in view. Like the openness of the Holy Grail, it explores a horizonless terrain, without a definitive end. Instead of a specific end, it is guided by an intention of Presence, an intention to arouse the energies of the heart and to extend them deep into a suffering world.

An awakened heart has leaped over the chasm between Self and Other; it is no longer Self-directed but rather Other-directed. In this view, there are no separations, no boundaries, no paths, no horizons, no permanent self, placing a limit on our capacity to love and care for others. It takes the humility and fearlessness of a Jumping Mouse—an Innocent Fool—to leap into the spacious freedom of this groundlessness.

Imagination: The Art of Dreaming

In its essence, The Story of Jumping Mouse illustrates the power of imagination to dream a new world into being. Little Mouse had to let go of his material and literal way of perceiving the world in order to see the Sacred Mountains. It was then that he began the journey into the vast spaciousness of his own heart, where he found the freedom of seeing with the eye of the heart.

It is imagination—the art of dreaming—that can carry us beyond the literal to the transcendent, beyond the concrete to the transparent, beyond ignorance to awakening. Through the lens of the imaginal, the heart sees clearly into the sorrows of the world and responds with care and compassion.

Contrary to what the literal-minded Old Mouse inside us says, the Sacred Mountains do exist. The longing in our hearts and our own ecstatic, poetic, ecological experience are testimony to this sacred reality. The decision to set out on the journey to the Sacred Mountains embodies the Quest. It brings the Quest to the center of our awareness; it brings awareness to the center of our Quest.

* * *

The Sacred Mountains rise up out of Mother Earth as a *vision place* from which we can see beyond all horizons to the Sacred Oneness of Life. From the Sacred Mountains we see Earth as a whole community of infinite life forms that weave themselves together through a relational dynamic into a single living mystery we call Life. We are immersed in a Great Mystery, from birth to death. Our rational minds can only skim its surface; to go deeper requires another kind of touching—one that arises from the heart of Communion and Care.

When we surrender to groundlessness, listening deeply, we can hear the roaring in our ears that is calling us out onto the Quest. The roaring is our ancestors' chanting at the edge of memory, reminding us of who we are.

Listen! The drums are beating and the singers are singing. The People are gathered in a circle in a glade in the foothills of the Sacred Mountains. The glade is surrounded by towering pine trees and dotted with wild flowers. The People are treating each other with respect and love. Love flows around the circle like a living current of energy uniting the hearts of The People into One Mind, One Heart, One Body. This love flows out, encompassing the trees, the grasses, the flowers, the mountains, the rivers, and the animals who share the Earth with them. Children play at the edges of the circle, their laughter like birdsong. The elders smile upon them and laugh, too. Mothers openly suckle their babies. Toddlers propel themselve pell-mell among the legs of The People. Adolescents stand in small groups flirting with each other. New arrivals are welcomed into the circle with smiles. They are all waiting but at ease.

Suddenly, their voices rise up in a cheer. Some of the adolescents are returning from their Vision Quests. They are welcomed back into the circle of community with open arms. They are showered with love. They are given gifts in recognition of the ordeal they have undergone so that The People may live. It is a good day to be alive. Overhead an eagle cries out. The People look up and smile. Great Spirit has blessed their circle.

* * *

The circle of Earth Community beckons to us from the other side of the threshold. It calls the Hero back home. The quest that began in solitude will end and begin again in the circle of community. The Hero will finally, after many centuries of lonely wandering, return to a troubled world with the long-awaited boon of an open heart.

Perhaps then, the great vision that the Oglala Lakota holy man Black Elk had as a young boy in the latter part of the 19th century may come to fruition. As Black Elk tells poet John Neihardt many years later, toward the end of his vision:

> … I was standing on the highest mountain of them all [Mount Harney in South Dakota], and round about beneath me was the whole hoop of the world. And while I stood there I saw more than I can tell and I understood more than I saw; for I was seeing in a sacred manner the shapes of all things in the spirit, and the shape

of all shapes as they must live together like one being. And I saw that the sacred hoop of my people was one of many hoops that made one circle, wide as daylight and as starlight, and in the center grew one mighty flowering tree to shelter all the children of one mother and one father. And I saw that it was holy.

The flowering tree stands in the center of the Medicine Wheel that turns at the center of the world. The Four Sacred Directions of the Medicine Wheel intersect in the human heart. The colorful prayer flags hanging from its branches flap in the wind, singing the songs of sorrow and joy that humanity has sung since time immemorial. To the heartbeat of Mother Earth, we dancers of Sun and Earth place our worries and burdens at its base, freeing our child's heart to sing songs of gratitude and joy.

As the radiant light emanating from this infinitely colored, flowering tree surrounds and fills us, our spirits soar with Eagle into freedom. Our trusting heart has found its wings. Like Jumping Mouse, we have emptied ourselves of our attachments to a separate self and to an already known world that blinds us from seeing clearly into the Original Nature of things; our hearts have opened wide enough to receive the whole world as a living mystery.

As in the symbolic dying of a Vision Quest, when you have reached the stillpoint of this emptiness, life magically reasserts itself through the void and a renewed appreciation of the beauty and wonder of life once again fills your heart. In this moment of emergence, an overwhelming sense of the sanctity of life and the blessedness of love becomes the heart river carrying you back into the sorrows of the world, with a renewed sense of resolve, care, and joy.

May our hearts become one heart river flowing into the soul of the world. May the soul of the world drink from our waters and be renewed. May all the beings of the world know freedom and rejoice.

Epilogue:

A Prayer for the Earth

May we take up the challenge
that is presented
in these dark times
May the Cry of the Earth
and all of her inhabitants
and the Cry of the People
those who have been cast out
because of the color of their skin
those who are poor, hungry, homeless
despairing of a dawn
incarcerated, angry, and lost
those young ones who cannot
find a home for their heart's longing
who have been numbed into a silent despair
May their cries be a roaring in our ears
May we awaken to the ways
we have forgotten who we are
and what destiny calls us forward
May the saving grace flow from the danger
that haunts our days
that screams from tree and rock
from bird and bear
from behind prison walls
from our bloody hands
How will it penetrate our numbness,
our narcissism and denial?
Who is listening?

Can we find the center place
where the heart knows no bounds
where we are brothers and sisters
who remember the forgotten Way In
who walk the holy road
of passion and beauty and love
whose eyes still light with wonder
who fall speechless before Mystery
who Care?
May the tears of Mother Earth melt
our hardened hearts
and the spirit of her children soar into our jaded
lives
and ignite the flame of longing and memory
carried forward by our Ancestors
                    —MITAKUYE OYASIN, ALL MY RELATIONS

Appendix:

A Medicine Wheel

*All things of the Universe Wheel have spirit and life, including the
rivers, rocks, earth, sky, plants and animals. But it is only man, of
all the Beings on the Wheel, who is a determiner. Our determining
spirit can be made whole only through the learning of our harmony
with all the other spirits of the universe. To do this we must learn
to seek and to perceive. We must do this to find our place within the
Medicine Wheel. To determine this place we must learn to Give-
Away.*

—*HYEMEYOHSTS STORM*

I learned this Medicine Wheel from my Vision Quest teachers, Meredith Little and
Steven Foster, who themselves learned it from a Nez Perce medicine man. This
particular Medicine Wheel originated in the Mayan culture in Mexico and eventually
was brought to North America by migrating tribes.

The Medicine Wheel symbolically represents a way of perceiving the Universe
and humanity's place within it. It is a cosmology that presents an ordered, harmonious
vision of the Universe.

The symbol for the Medicine Wheel is a circle divided into four quadrants—a
universal symbol for wholeness, which can also be found in the Celtic cross and Buddhist mandalas. The Medicine Wheel is regarded as a symbolic representation of the
Great Circle of Life, which contains all that exists within its embrace—plants, trees,
animals, humans, rivers, stones, earth, sky, stars, moon, sun, and so on. Just like the
Great Medicine Lake in our story, it is a mirror reflecting all the beings and powers of
the natural world. Importantly, within the spiritual ecology of the Medicine Wheel,
humans are viewed as an integral part of the whole, neither greater nor lesser than any
other part and inseparably connected to every other part.

Each quadrant on the Medicine Wheel represents one of the four cardinal directions, and each direction is associated with one of the four elements: South/Earth,

West/Water, North/Air, and East/Fire. Each direction is also linked to a season: South/Summer, West/Fall, North/Winter, and East/Spring. Additionally, since Nature is a mirror of the human soul, each direction represents a dimension or aspect of being human, as well as a stage in human development: South/Body/Child; West/Soul or Psyche/Adolescent; North/Mind/Adult; and East/Spirit/Death and Rebirth. Each direction has an animal associated with it: South/Mouse, West/Bear, North/Buffalo, and East/Eagle. Finally each direction has a corresponding color: South/Red, West/Black, North/White, and East/Yellow or Gold.

To the native way of perceiving, the Four Sacred Directions represent elemental powers of Nature; as such, they are also referred to as the Four Winds. They are the primordial and irreducible forces that brought about the creation of Earth and life itself. These powers inform all of life and, as such, are greater than any single manifestation of life. Although they can be harnessed by us to serve our needs, these powers, like the wind, are greater than our attempts to control them.

The powers of the directions play a role in human psychology and, in this regard, are known as The Four Shields or Faces of Human Nature. "Shields," in this instance, are not to be understood solely as instruments of protection—although they can certainly serve that purpose—but are regarded primarily as Nature's powers reflected in human nature.

Each of us is born predisposed toward a way of perceiving the world characteristic of one of the directions. But as a seeker in quest of the Sacred Mountains each person seeks to integrate the aspects of the other less developed ways of perceiving. The quest is a way to turn the Medicine Wheel and to bring the powers of the directions into greater balance and harmony within the person. When an individual develops and integrates each of the four faces of being human—Body, Mind, Psyche, and Spirit—the individual stands in the center of the Medicine Wheel with a wide open heart that embraces the full range of human experience and all the beings that share this beautiful Earth with us. It is then, as the Navajo say, that the individual walks the Beauty Way.

The Medicine Wheel also tells the developmental story of the human journey through the stages of life: childhood, adolescence, adulthood, and death. Metaphors of transformation as depicted in the cycle of the changing seasons tell this story. In this way of seeing, the human soul is understood and revealed in the mirror of Nature in terms of an intimate interconnectedness and communion with the elemental and cyclical forces of the natural world.

This communion is not implicit in our experience, as it is with other animals who instinctively live the harmony from birth. Graced with self-reflective consciousness, humans are engaged in a quest through which we may learn of our harmony with other beings.

The South

Little Mouse in our story begins his journey in the South. He finds himself, as each of us does, born into a body on this Earth and immersed in the collective body of a family, tribe, community, or nation.

The South represents the locus of Mother Earth and her powers of giving birth to, nurturing, and sustaining life in all its wonderful complexity and diversity. To the native mind, the Earth as Mother is a living being in possession of a soul and spirit, and she must always be respected and honored as sacred. She is the sacred ground we walk upon. This is an ancient view, which is universally present among indigenous peoples ranging from Siberia to South America, and also among the pagan Goddess religions of our Western European heritage and the Celts.

The life-sustaining abundance of Mother Earth feeds us and our animal brothers and sisters. The body of the Earth, matter itself, is transmuted into the blood, bones, and flesh of our own bodies. Quite literally, the body of the Earth and our bodies are one. The plants and trees that carpet her surface give off the oxygen without which there would be no life. The rich nutrients of her body feed the plants that provide food for animals and humans. The waters that course through her interior and emerge as springs, rivers, and lakes are the source from which we all drink. Her plant medicines heal us from wounds and sickness. Her trees frame our living structures and her plants clothe us. Her wood, oil, and natural gas heat our dwellings. Her beauty feeds our souls and inspires us to new levels of vision.

Our inescapable unity and interdependence with Mother Earth signifies her as our original home. She is literally the ground upon which we stand and spiritually the sacred landscape that mirrors our souls and inspires us to reach for the divine. Without her we are lost; with her we are rooted and whole; in prayer and gratitude to her we are holy.

The season associated with this life-giving aspect of Mother Earth is summer. During the summer, the world is enlivened by warm winds, the light of the sun, and life-giving rains. New plants and animals grow rapidly in summer's embrace. The world is lush with colors—green vegetation and a rich palette of flowers. Mother Earth displays her fertility and freely supports all life in its many manifestations. Likewise, at the interface of the natural world with the human world within the Medicine Wheel, summer is the growing fields of the child.

In an ideal family environment, the child is allowed to play freely in all innocence and trust. As the psychologist Erik Erikson states in *Identity and the Life Cycle*, the healthy development of a personality is dependent upon establishing a "basic trust" in others and oneself in the first year of life. Eventually, as the child matures, this basic trust will be extended from the maternal matrix to the matrix of the natural world, and eventually on to the world at large.

The establishment of this basic trust at home and in Nature allows the child to develop in a healthy way and to freely express the full range of her emotions. The sweet innocence of childhood appears as though the nectar of the gods and goddesses has become distilled in the child's overflowing heart. The child experiences and expresses wholeheartedly joy, wonder, spontaneity, play, and unconditional love. These qualities of being are also fully available to the adult who has not lost connection with the child in the South.

Some children, however, may survive a difficult childhood by closing off this shield. Lacking a basic trust in life because of wounds to their integrity, these children undergo a numbing of their emotional life that protects them from feeling the full force of the pain or terror that dwells in their hearts. As adults, their task will be to open up this shield in order to bring the flowing river of their emotions back into their life. They will need to learn to feel again and to trust the world.

Other children may survive a difficult childhood by getting stuck in the South shield. In this case, the child becomes the victim of raging emotions such as temper tantrums they cannot control, and as an adult they are subject to hysterical emotional flooding. As adults, their task will be to develop the powers of the North shield in order to tame and channel these raw emotions into constructive and creative modes of expression.

Whether nurtured with love or abused, a child can also give vent to the darker emotions of fear, anger, rage, jealousy, possessiveness, and even hatred. The raw emotions of the child have not yet been tempered through experience and awareness. The child still lives in primary process, close to her instinctual nature. Of course, as adults we too can be taken over by these raw emotions to the point where they control us rather than we control them. In the extreme, these unchecked, negative emotions of the South can suddenly erupt into aggression, violence, and, on a global scale, war. In this we give expression to the potential for violence also present within the South shield, as we engage in an instinctual, fear-driven struggle for survival and a competitive advantage.

If this direction could be reduced to one statement, it would be "I want." The child is an impulsive body of wants and needs that demand immediate satisfaction; he has not yet learned to temper his appetites with discipline. With respect to the adult, if the appetites of the South can be moderated, however, the body can remain healthy and the mind sane.

It is when the appetites and immature desires of the ego-body reign supreme that they can be a destructive force. Their self-destructive manifestations include addictions, greed, and blind ambition. Undisciplined by awareness, these desires feed upon themselves and can never be truly satisfied. Most of us in our consumer-oriented society have probably been caught up at one time or another in the treadmill of desire, such that shortly after we have attained some much valued object of desire we find ourselves feeling unsatisfied again and desiring something else to fill the void. The problem is that we innocently, like a child, pin our happiness on the attainment of some ephemeral external pleasure or object. The impulsivity of such immature desires leads only to an increase in our suffering and not to happiness, and in the long run is harmful to self, relationships, society, and the Earth. Significantly, however, these immature desires, like the ripples on an ocean, are a superficial expression of much deeper human desires that require a certain degree of health and awareness to manifest. Some of these would be a desire for love, beauty, community, and wholeness.

The body of the South is also the conduit through which the physical world is experienced. Physical reality in all its wonderful, sensuous display delights and lures us into sensual contact. Through sight, sound, smell, touch, and taste our inseparable connection and interdependence with the physical world is affirmed and celebrated in each moment. The body is our organ of relational communion with what is Other. The body as the house of our sensuality and sexuality likewise draws us into the intimate embrace of the Other. The life-giving red blood that animates our bodies moves us out of the isolation of a self-enclosed subjectivity, ignites our passions, and opens our hearts toward a more abundant expression of our life force. Here the color red, symbolic of the South, is associated with the heart, which moves us through emotion (e-motion) to act, to care, to love, and to create.

Each direction is also represented by an animal. The South is the province of mouse. He is the incessantly busy one with his nose to the ground and constantly vigilant. If the mouse part of ourselves prevails, then fear dominates our perception of reality. Caught up in the struggle for survival and security, our perception of reality can be severely restricted by what we see directly in front of us. Immediate material reality is the only thing that is thought to be real; the Sacred Mountains are thought of as merely a myth, as Old Mouse states in our story.

In our constant search for security, we can also become hoarders of things. Out of fear, we cling to material objects, people, assumptions, beliefs, biases, judgments, resentments, psychological wounds, and habitual patterns of thinking, feeling, and acting. This tendency represents an unconscious attempt to realize certainty and security in an uncertain world.

From a Buddhist perspective, when the energies of the South shield become extreme and negative, manifesting as fear, immature desire, blind ambition, impulsivity, and an exclusive attachment to material reality, they define the world of *samsara*, a world of suffering caused by an endless search for security and by an ignorance of our true nature. The Buddhist sees this world of samsara as an illusion beclouding an awareness of our basic goodness of heart and of our innate capacity to be fully and fearlessly awake in each moment, without clinging to the past or worrying about the future.

Paradoxically, the South contains the seeds of both of these possibilities. Suspended between fear and trust, we have a choice in each moment whether to suffer the pain of our habitual patterns of reactive emotions and negativity, or to realize a joyful participation in the wonders and sorrows of the world.

The West

The element associated with the West is water. Water, along with fire, is the element most closely associated with transformation. From a mythological perspective, as the sun sets in the West it sinks into the dark waters of its night-sea journey, just as, analogously, humans descend in sleep into the dark waters of the unconscious. The waters of the unsconscious are the source of creative imagination and help us dream the world into being.

As the place of the setting sun and the darkness that follows, the color associated with the West is black. The sun-filled days of summer give way to the shorter days and longer nights of fall. The exuberant extroversion of summer yields to the quiet introversion of fall. The West is the Looks-Within place, the place of introspection. It is a dying-back time, a retreat into the womb of inwardness and darkness, a period of dormancy within which the life forces can rest, recharge, and in some cases undergo a transformation.

In terms of the development of the human soul, adolescence is the prototypical time of inwardness and transformation. In adolescence, the innocence and trust of the child comes face to face with the suffering that can attend the maturation process and initiate a turn inward. It may arrive with an adolescent's experiences of betrayal, rejection, loss of love, alienation, depression, longing, and so on. For many young people, adolescence can be a dark time—a fall from innocence. During adolescence, we are searching to find our own identity as distinct from our parents and family. Everything is thrown into question, including the values and beliefs of our family and culture. The Quest begins.

Often there is a barely conscious longing for God, or whatever word we give to that which is greater than the merely human, as the adolescent looks directly across the Medicine Wheel to the East, the dwelling place of Spirit. This longing can find expression in a search for an experience of nonordinary reality, with or without drugs.

So the adolescent can suffer as they make this self-reflective turn inward, just as Bear, the animal associated with this direction, in late fall seeks a den to hibernate in for the winter. This introspective turn signals the birth of psychological consciousness, a descent into psyche or the soul. The primary narcissism of the child gives way to the adolescent's budding self-awareness and sense of responsibility. With the awakening of self-consciousness, adolescents take things inside and learn how to communicate their feelings. Rather than reacting angrily, like a child, they have a choice to say, "I feel angry." And, equally important, in adolescence the raw emotions of the child can be refined into tender, subtle feelings; the heart opens wide to beauty and love, and becomes acutely sensitive to insult. Indeed, if the essence of adolescence could be reduced to one statement, it would be "I feel." It is in adolescence that we perhaps fall in love for the first time, have strong feelings about topics important to us, and are passionately idealistic. And these feelings can be turbulent and changing, like the waters of the ocean.

Riding out these storms of questions and feelings can be difficult, especially if, as in our culture, there are few mentors to whom adolescents can turn for guidance. Indeed, sometimes they fall apart, falling into depression, or thoughts of suicide, if not acts; or they engage in self-destructive and numbing behaviors, such as drug and alcohol abuse, promiscuity, and dangerous risk-taking; or, as is becoming an increasingly familiar story today, they lash out against themselves and the world through violence.

From an indigenous perspective, many of these behaviors are misguided attempts at initiation. These kids are crying out for initiation into adulthood, but there is no one there to respond to their dire need. So they do it themselves, unconsciously and ineffectually.

The difficult times some young people go through may turn out to be a particularly Western means of stepping through the door into initiation and transformation. Transformation always takes place in a confrontation with the unknown. If you remain on known ground, all the old attitudes, beliefs, defenses, and habits remain in place, and nothing changes. When you face the unknown, you begin the mythic underworld journey of the hero/heroine and rebirth becomes a possibility.

The indigenous mind knows of the pitfalls and possibilities intrinsic to the adolescent passage into adulthood. Thus, these cultures respond to this significant time with formal rites of passage, which are an initiation into the deep mysteries of the human soul and of life. It is in the West that we undertake the quest to discover our true nature.

The North

The North is informed by the element of air. The invisible movements of air are the living breath that animates all life. All life forms on the Earth exchange breath with each other to form an invisible web of life energy; we breath together as one body. The breath of the deer that silently passes by my house at night is inhaled by me and my family as we lay sleeping and perhaps dreaming of deer. The trees of the forests around the world are our breathing companions as they inhale our exhaled carbon dioxide and exhale life-supporting oxygen. Air is also the medium that carries sound to our ears; as such, it makes possible the manifold ways humans and animals communicate with each other, and thus is crucial in the formation of relationship and community.

Mind is associated with air because of its capacity for abstraction and its ability to process information with such amazing speed and versatility. In its purest cosmological form, mind can be envisioned as the universal intelligence that underlies all creation. In its human distillation, mind manifests as wisdom. In Western thought, wisdom refers to the capacity of the mind to discern what is true, good, right, and beautiful.

In making decisions, the wisdom of the mind does not rely exclusively upon reason; rather, it seeks to incorporate the lessons of the heart. Genuine wisdom issues forth from a balanced mind—a mind that marries reason (logos) and the heart (eros). A balanced mind stands in the heart center of the Medicine Wheel, in the middle ground between reason (North shield) and passion (South shield). It is a disciplined mind that neither reacts impulsively to the self-centered desires of the moment, nor stifles the soft murmurs of the heart with a merciless logic. Mind as pure awareness is the greatest gift we humans have been given. Pure awareness is Spirit—Spirit is pure awareness.

The North is the place of the season of winter. Its color is the pure white of freshly fallen snow. The element of air dominates, as the fierce, frigid, purifying winds of the North blow across the desolate landscape. All plant life has retreated into itself, most birds have migrated south, only the mammals remain to struggle through a time of scarcity and endurance.

To endure a winter in the North requires strength, courage, and perseverance. Buffalo, the animal associated with this direction, shows the people how to walk with power and endurance, "facing the great white cleansing wind of the world." Animals and people alike must strip down to what is essential for survival. For people living close to the land, survival in the winter in the North requires intelligence, planning, and cooperation in the form of a community banded together for the common good. It requires wisdom—a balanced mind that is capable of making decisions that will ensure the survival and well-being of the community.

In terms of the soul's journey around the Medicine Wheel, having descended into the darkness of initiation, the boy or girl emerges reborn into his manhood or her womanhood in the North. Having undergone the rigors of initiation, they are no longer children and must now wear the mantle of full adult responsibility. Later, as they mature into genuine elders, they are those adults who have been purified and stripped of their self-importance and self-centeredness by the purifying winds of initiation, suffering, and experience. In the words of Fools Crow, a great Oglala Sioux medicine man, they have become a "hollow bone" through which Spirit may flow unobstructed into the world.

They have come into the fullness of their manhood and womanhood; they are genuine elders, a title not based on age but rather on a demonstrated integrity, humility, wisdom, and compassion. As elders, the immediate and long-range care of the community is their first priority. Each decision is measured against its impact on not just the present community but the seventh generation to come. If the essence of this direction could be reduced to one statement, it would be "I care." In the spirit of the Give-Away, exemplified by the revered Buffalo, the elders selflessly give away themselves for the sake of the tribe. They selflessly place their ego on the altar of community.

The elders of the North, then, play a critical role within the structure of the community as the guardians of the sacred—the keepers of wisdom. As such, they are the ones who tend the sacred fires that unite the community into One Mind. This One Mind is not to be confused with the modern phenomena of mass conformity; rather, it represents the spiritual alignment of each individual within the tribe with Great Spirit and the welfare of the whole.

Like each of the other directions, the North shield also contains its shadow side. The shadow side of the mind displays itself when we fall under the illusion that we are separate from each other and use this belief to distance ourselves from or inflict suffering on others. This, of course, is *the* fundamental illusion that we all live. This divisive and isolating tendency appears in us when our fearful ego becomes rigid and defensive in its thinking and resists change at all costs. In our fear, we exhibit a façade of hubris, which Plato regarded as the most destructive weakness of the human soul.

We witness this, perhaps most strikingly, in the narrow-minded, rigid either-or thinking of religious fundamentalists, who say that their way is the only right way and that those who disagree with them are evil. This way of thinking has been and continues to be a major, if not *the* major, source of conflict in the world, leading to wars, genocide, and other violent acts against humanity.

But each of us is highly susceptible to our own brand of fundamentalism. Out of fear and a need for something solid to hold onto in a complex, ambiguous, rapidly changing world each of us can cling to cherished beliefs. Each of us experiences times when we take ourselves all too seriously and harden our hearts to the Other. When we do so, we lose the softening connection to the heart of the child in the South and forget how to trust and laugh and play. We sacrifice a sense of wonder before the astounding diversity, beauty, and mystery of the Universe, for the sake of a false certainty and a flimsy sense of authority.

Authentic elders, on the other hand, develop and maintain the flow of energies along the North-South axis of the Medicine Wheel. They keep the child alive in their heart and are able to laugh at themselves. They have learned how to dance on the bones of their cherished beliefs and attitudes. This North-South connection is the central axis around which the Medicine Wheel turns.

When we become too rigid and self-righteous as adults, we are unable to respond adequately to the suffering of the adolescent and consequently cannot be genuine mentors to them. When this happens, it is usually because we are in denial regarding our own suffering, past and present. At its deepest level, we are in denial of our own death. In denial, we attach ourselves to illusory certainties, beliefs, and either-or moralities, which only serve to separate us farther from others and to drive the young person deeper into alienation.

To embody the powers of the true elder in the North, we need to embrace the powers of the other directions—the sense of innocence and trust of the child in the South, the introspection and feeling of the adolescent in the West, and the illuminating vision of the East. Only in this way can we realize balance, harmony, wisdom, and beauty on the sacred path.

The East

Fire is the elemental power that prevails in the East. The Toltecs of Mexico regard Grandfather Fire as the most powerful force in the Universe. In many creation myths the world was created from fire. We need only think of our own scientific origin story of the Big Bang. Also, there is the fire contained within the nuclear core of an atom, an awesome power for both creation and destruction. Moreover, at the core of the Earth there is a molten fire, which in turn is mirrored in the fire of the sun, without whose warmth, light, and energy there would be no life on Earth.

According to the Toltecs, we are children of the sun, and we are meant to shine. The fire of the sun burns inside each of us. It is this fire that ignites our quests for vision and awakening. It is this fire in the East that adolescents in the West turn their longing hearts toward, like a flower to the sun.

When we entered the western portal of the Medicine Wheel, we crossed over the threshold into the mystery of the dark: the mystery of initiation, transformation, and death. Now here in the East we enter the mystery of light: the mystery of illumination, enlightenment, ecstasy, and rebirth. This light is the counterpart to the darkness, for we cannot have one without the other in the mysterious symmetry of the Universe.

If all goes well on the heroic night-sea journey of the soul, the soul reemerges in the East beneath the blazing fire of The Great Eastern Sun. The courageous journey through the dark to its end—not avoiding, denying, dismissing, or trying to fix it—eventually brings the soul to the light and promise of renewal and rebirth.

In terms of our life journey on the Medicine Wheel, eventually the elder grows old and dies. Death reclaims life. But life is not totally extinguished, because out of death comes new life, just as out of the dying of winter the warmth and light of spring returns to the land to spark a rebirth; just as out of the dying of the plant a seed lies in the ground awaiting the right conditions to germinate into new life. The cycle of life, death, and rebirth continues around the Medicine Wheel and within our own psyches, marking the cosmic and transpersonal cadence of renewal and transformation.

The East is the Otherworld of Spirit—the transpersonal, eternal realm, beyond space and time, yet paradoxically immanent in all things. The words and images that we use to name it—words such as God and Great Spirit—cannot reach it; they are merely signposts pointing beyond themselves toward that which is ineffable. If we get stuck in the words and images, we will be unable to leap ecstatically into the mystery that surrounds us each moment of our lives. As the Zen Buddhists say, "If you see the Buddha on the road, kill him." This is a caution to the spiritual seeker to watch out for the tendency to turn a person or a symbol into an object of worship, as opposed to realizing that divinity within one's own heart.

As the place of the rising sun and the new dawn, the East is associated with the rebirth of life in the spring. It is the source of the eternal fire that turns the Medicine Wheel and fuels our inspiration, creativity, illumination, and vision. The morning light of the Great Eastern Sun, as a symbol of this illuminating power, dispels the night darkness and brings with it the promise of renewal and vision. The East is the direction that carries the Possible into our lives on the wings of the far-seeing eagle.

Eagle, whose flight reaches the highest in the blue dome of sky, is regarded by native people as a messenger of Great Spirit, an intermediary between Spirit and humans. It is the vision of Eagle that carries us, in ever-expanding orbits, beyond the horizon of our ignorance and attachments, our wounds and pettiness, our fears and defenses, our self-importance and self-centered desires. It is through the eye of Eagle that vision and illumination enters our hearts. It is through the Eye of the Heart that the invisible becomes manifest in the visible.

Mythologically, it is the vision of the ones who go to the Sacred Mountains that serves to regenerate the community that has succumbed to an inevitable winter dieback. It is to the light in the East that we turn in search of guidance when we have fallen into despair and hopelessness. It is the light in the East that guides the adolescent as he wanders through the dark forest, in the threshold space between time and eternity, between the world and Spirit. It is around the Sacred Fire Circle that the community renews its bonds and celebrates life's gifts and mysteries in ritual.

The Way of Beauty

We have circumnavigated the Medicine Wheel beginning in the South and ending in the East. However, like the alchemical symbol of the dragon biting its own tail (the Uroboros), the Medicine Wheel has no beginning and no end; it is a constantly turning, ever-repeating, ever-evolving dynamic that flies in the face of fixed categories and definitive ends.

In the native way of perceiving, as represented in the Medicine Wheel, humans derive their Medicine Power by virtue of the ways through which they attune to, participate in, honor, and celebrate the life-giving interdependence and sacredness of all living things. Traditional native people realize power by entering into an intimate relationship with an ensouled world that is animated by a spiritual force greater than the human. Their lives are centered around seeking ways to come into communion with this force.

The relational orientation of the Medicine Wheel reveals itself most strongly and beautifully in the central place that the West shield plays in its dynamism. The Vision Quest places individuals in the heart of Nature, where they come face to face with the mystery of their own soul and the soul of the world. In that encounter a person forges a relationship with the hidden possibilities within his or her soul.

All the teachings of the native way are geared toward creating opportunities for an individual to form such relationships of mutual reciprocity and partnership with Spirit as revealed in Nature.

To form a relationship and partnership with Nature is to see with the Eye of the Heart and to know intimately the full context of the relational world in which one finds oneself. It is to move within the heart circle of touching and being touched with respect, reverence, and gratitude. It is to walk on the Earth with an abiding sense of beauty, a sense of the cosmic order and goodness. It is to move from the heart center of the Medicine Wheel outward in concentric rings of relational depth, richness, inclusion, and loving care. It is to walk the Way of Beauty through the joys and sorrows of the world.

The following words of Black Elk capture the heart of walking the Way of Beauty:

> I am blind and do not see the things of this world; but when the
> Light comes from Above, it enlightens my heart and I can see, for
> the Eye of my heart sees everything. The heart is a sanctuary at
> the center of which there is a little space, wherein the Great Spirit
> dwells, and this is the Eye. This is the Eye of the Great Spirit by
> which He sees all things and through which we see Him.
> …In order to know the center of the heart where Great Spirit
> dwells you must be pure and good, and live in the manner that the
> Great Spirit has taught us. The man who is thus pure contains the
> Universe in the pocket of his heart.

May each of us find the Beauty Way and see with the eye of the heart into the heart of a suffering world.

NOTES

"The Tower Beyond Tragedy," poem from *The Collected Poetry of Robinson Jeffers volume 1*, edited by Tim Hunt. Copyright © 1938 by Garth and Donnan Jeffers; renewed 1966. All rights reserved. Used with the permission of Stanford University Press, www.sup.org.

Introduction

Steven Foster and Meredith Little, *The Roaring of the Sacred River: The Wilderness Quest for Vision and Self-Healing* (Big Pine, CA: Lost Borders Press, 1989).
"touching" is from Hyemeyohsts Storm, *Seven Arrows* (New York: Ballantine Books, 1972), 7.

PART ONE – Separation:
A Glimpse of the Sacred Mountains

"The power that is there for the healing of our world..." from "The Power of Grief," by Joanna Macy, in *Earth & Spirit, The Spiritual Dimension of the Environmental Crisis*, 182.

CHAPTER 1: The Call of the Unknown

"The *Vision Quest*, or perceiving quest, is the way..." is from Storm's *Seven Arrows*, 5.
"Indigenous people are indigenous..." is from Somé's *Ritual: Power, Healing and Community*, 33.
"Call to Adventure" is from Joseph Campbell, *The Hero with a Thousand Faces*, 49.
Reference: Wirrarika people of Mexico is from Victor Sanchez, *Toltecs of the New Millennium*.
David Whyte, "The Well of Grief," *Where Many Rivers Meet*, © Many Rivers Press, Langley, Washington. Printed with permission from Many Rivers Press, *www.davidwhyte.com*.
"How Much is Not True," *The Kabir Book* by Robert Bly. Copyright © 1971, 1977 by Robert Bly. © 1977 by the Seventies Press. Reprinted by permission of Beacon Press, Boston.
Reference: "midwife to the soul..." is from Foster & Little, *The Roaring of the Sacred River*, 6.
this "circular dynamic..." is from Cowan, *Fire in the Head: Shamanism and the Celtic Spirit*, 13.
Reference: The Dalai Lama on absence of self-hatred in his culture is from "Sitting in the Fire: Pema Chodron on Turning Toward Pain," an interview by James Kulkander in *The Sun*, Issue 349, January 2005. Also see His Holiness the Dalai Lama & Howard C. Cutler, M.D., *The Art of Happiness: A Handbook for Living* (New York: Riverhead Books, 1998), 283.
Reference: Buddhist concept of basic goodness see Chogyam Trungpa, *Shambhala: The Sacred Path of the Warrior*.
"When we say the Okanagan word for ourselves..." is from Jeanette Armstrong, "I Stand with You Against the Disorder," *Yes!*, Winter 2006.
Chellis Glendinning on post-traumatic stress disorder see *My Name is Chellis and I'm in Recovery from Western Civilization*, 22-26.
"... to be desirable..." is from "Anima Mundi: The Return of the Soul to the World" by James Hillman in *Spring Journal* (1982), 88-89.
"[their] Christ nature, that is [their] individuation process..." is from Johnson, *He: Understanding Masculine Psychology*, 9-10.

"one on top of the other in the round…" is from Erich Neumann, *The Origins and History of Consciousness*, 8.

CHAPTER 2: Rites of Passage: An Archetypal Blueprint

"… there is a thinking in primordial images…" is from Carl Jung, *Modern Man In Search of a Soul* (Routledge Classics, 2005), 115.

Reference: "monomyth" is from Campbell, *The Hero with a Thousand Faces*.

Reference: threefold structure found among indigenous people is from van Gennep, *Rites of Passage*.

"Nature shows itself in some unique way…" "The Healing Power of Nature," from *The Healing Wisdom of Africa*, by Malidoma Patrice Somé, copyright © 1998 by Malidoma Patrice Somé. Used by permission of Jeremy P. Tarcher, an imprint of Penguin Group (USA) Inc.

Mircea Eliade, *Rites and Symbols of Initiation: The Mysteries of Birth and Rebirth*, 3.

Lost Borders: Coming of age in the Wilderness, produced and directed by Kim Shelton, Two Shoes Productions, 1998, (distributed by Bullfrog Films). Also see Paul Shepard, *Nature and Madness* (San Francisco: Sierra Club Books, 1982)

250,000 adolescents attempt suicide is from the Web site of the National Institute of Mental Health, "Depression in Children and Adolescents: A Fact Sheet for Physicians, *www.nimh.nih.gov/publicat/depchildresfact.cfm.*

"In tribal cultures, it was said that if boys were not initiated…" is from Michael Meade, *Men and the Water of Life: Initiation and the Tempering of Men*, 19.

CHAPTER 3: Stories from the Threshold: A Wilderness Rite of Passage for Adolescents

A version of this chapter first appeared as "Exploring Second Nature: Youth, Wilderness, & Rites of Initiation," in *Earthlight: The Magazine of Spiritual Ecology*, Winter 2002/Issue 4.

PART TWO – Initiation:
Journey to the Sacred Mountains

"Perhaps the most important reason for lamenting…" from *Indian Spirit,* edited by Michael Oren Fitzgerald, 21.

CHAPTER 4: The Old Mouse: A Failure of Imagination

I jotted down this quote from Camus years ago without noting the reference. My guess would be *The Rebel*.

"Dich wundert nicht…/You are not surprised…", Ich war bei den altesten…/I was there with the first…", from Rilke's *Book Of Hours: Love Poems To God* by Rainer Maria Rilke, translated by Anita Barrows and Joanna Macy, copyright © 1996 by Anita Barrows and Joanna Macy. Used by permission of Riverhead Books, an imprint of Penquin Group (USA) Inc.

Joseph Bruchac, *Native American Stories: Told by Joseph Bruchac* (Golden, CO: Fulcrum Publishing, 1991), 109.

"The Way In" (p.71) from *Selected Poems Of Rainer Maria Rilke*, A Translation From The German And Commentary By Robert Bly. Copyright © 1981 by Robert Bly. Reprinted by permission of HarperCollins Publishers.

"We have to use Imagination…" is from William Irwin Thompson, *The Time Falling Bodies Take to Light* (St. Martin's Press, 1981), 102.

See Robert Lawlor, *Voices of the First Day: Awakening in the Aboriginal Dreamtime* (Rochester, VT: Inner Traditions, 1991 and Bruce Chatwin, *The Songlines* (New York: Penquin Books, 1987).

Knowing as gnosis see Robert Avens, *The New Gnosis* (Dallas, TX: Spring Publications, 1984).

"transforming attention" is from Anita Barrows and Joanna Macy, "Introduction," in *Rilke's Book of Hours: Love Poems to God* (New York: Riverhead Books, 1996).

Reference to Mayans singing the world into existence is from "Saving the Indigenous Soul: An Interview with Martin Prechtel," by Derrick Jensen, *The Sun,* April 2001.

"The gesture acquires meaning…" is from Mircea Eliade, *Cosmos and History: The Myth of the Eternal Return* (New York: Harper & Rowe, 1959), 5.

Reference to us moderns being swept up in the rush of history is from Paul Shepard, *Coming Home to the Pleistocene* (Washington, D. C.: Island Press, 1998), 14-15.

"poetic basis of mind…" is from James Hillman, *Revisioning Psychology* (New York: Harper & Row, 1975), xi.

"A sacramental bond between our earliest human ancestors…" is from Monica Sjoo and Barbara Mor, *The Great Cosmic Mother*, 80.

Joanna Macy, *Despair and Personal Power in the Nuclear Age* (Philadelphia: New Society, 1983).

"autism" is from Thomas Berry, "Into the Future," in *Earth and Spirit: The Spiritual Dimension of the Environmental Crisis* (edited by Fritz Hull, New York: Continuum, 1993).

CHAPTER 5: The Buffalo: The Spirit of the Give-Away

"A human being is a part of the whole…" from a letter Albert Einstein wrote.

Joseph Epes Brown, ed., *The Sacred Pipe: Black Elk's Account of the Seven Sacred Rites of the Oglala Sioux* (Norman, OK: University of Oklahoma Press).

"In the history of symbols this tree…" is from Carl Jung, *The Archetypes and the Collective Unconscious* (Princeton, NJ: Princeton University Press, 1980), 110.

Joseph Campbell, *The Mythic Image* (Princeton, NJ: Princeton University Press, 1974), 198.

"[The] steady, strong beat [of the drum] is the pulse…" is from Joseph Epes Brown, *Sacred Pipe,* 69.

"When we go to the center of the hoop…" is from Brown, *Sacred Pipe,* 85.

"This truth of the oneness of all things…" is from Brown, *Sacred Pipe,* 95.

"My greatest Medicine is One of the Mind, the Body, and the Heart…" is from Storm, *Seven Arrows,* 243.

"Within the bewildering maelstrom of thoughts and emotions…" is from *Turning the Mind into and Ally* by Sakyong Mipham, © 2003 by Mipham J. Mukpo. Used by permission of The Berkley Publishing Group (Riverhead Books), a division of Penquin Group (USA) Inc., 165.

CHAPTER 6: Wolf: Guide to the Sacred Mountains

"Enlightenment is not a light that enables you to discover…" is from Bradford Keeney, *Shaking Out the Spirits: A Psychotherapist's Entry into the Healing Mysteries of Global Shamanism* (Barrytown, New York: Station Hill Press, 1994), 63.

"nonabiding awakening" is from Adyashanti, *The End of Your World* (Sounds True, 2008), 5-8.

For more on the Triple Goddess see Monica Sjoo and Barbara Mor, *The Great Cosmic Mother* and Kathie Carlson, *Life's Daughter/Death's Bride.*

CHAPTER 7: Eagle: Flight into Freedom

"There is a very important distinction between transformation and change..." is from Pema Chodron, *Tonglen: The Path of Transformation* (Halifax, Canada: Vajradhatu Publications, 2001), 77-78.

"Our deepest fear is not that we are inadequate..." is from Marianne Williamson, *A Return to Love* (Harper Collins, 1992).

"radical acceptance" is from Tara Brach, *Radical Acceptance: Embracing Your Life with the Heart of the Buddha* (New York: Bantam Books, 2003).

"Last Night," from *Times Alone: Selected Poems of Antonio Machado,* translated by Robert Bly, Wesleyan University Press, 1983. Used by permission from Robert Bly.

The discussion of death draws from Stephen Batchelor, *Buddhism Without Beliefs: A Contemporary Guide to Awakening* (New York: Penguin Putnam, 1997), 28-33.

"It seemed, so great my happiness/That I was blessed and could bless." Reprinted with the permission of Scribner, a Division of Simon & Schuster, Inc. from *The Collected Works Of W.B. Yeats, Volume I: The Poems, Revised,* edited by Richard J. Finneran. Copyright © 1933 by The Macmillan Company; copyright renewed © 1961 by Bertha Georgie Yeats. All rights reserved.

The Firebird is taken from Meade, *Men and the Water of Life,* 209.

"Ironically, this alienated self-centeredness..." is from *Buddhism Without Beliefs* by Stephen Batchelor, copyright © 1997 by Stephen Batchelor & The Buddhist Ray, Inc. Used by permission of Riverhead Books, an imprint of Penquin Group (USA) Inc., 95.

"Reality is intrinsically free..." is from *Buddhism Without Beliefs,* 99.

PART THREE – Incorporation:
Walking the Pathless Path Between Worlds

"The Anarchy of the Gaps", from *Living With The Devil* by Stephen Batchelor, copyright © 2004 by Stephan Batchelor. Used by permission of Riverhead Books, an imprint of Penquin Group (USA) Inc.

CHAPTER 9: A Culture at the Threshold

From *Myths To Live By* by Joseph Campbell, copyright © 1972 by Joseph Campbell. Used by permission of Viking Penquin, a division of Penquin Group (USA) Inc.

On the "great turning" see Joanna Macy and Molly Young Brown, *Coming Back to Life* (Gabriola Island: B.C.: New Society Publishers, 1998); Thomas Berry, *The Great Work: Our Way into the Future* (New York: Bell Tower, 1999); and David C. Korten, *The Great Turning: From Empire to Earth Community* (Berrett-Koehler Publishers: San Francisco and Kumarian Press: Bloomfield, CT).

"There I was standing on the highest mountain..." is from Nicholas Black Elk, *Black Elk Speaks, as told through John G. Neihardt (Flaming Rainbow)* (Lincoln, Nebraska: University of Nebraska Press, 2002), 33.

The image of the flowering tree was influenced by the reading of Robert Thurman's *The Jewel Tree of Tibet: The Enlightenment Engine of Tibetan Buddhism* (New York: Free Press, 2005).

Five lines of "*The Invitation*" {"I want to know if you can get up/... to feed the children."} from *The Invitation* by Oriah Mountain Dreamer. Copyright © 1999 by Oriah Mountain Dreamer. Reprinted by permission of HarperCollins Publishers.

APPENDIX: A Medicine Wheel

Storm, *Seven Arrows*, 5.

I learned about this Medicine Wheel from Steven Foster and Meredith Little. Also see Steven Foster and Meredith Little, *The Four Shields: The Initiatory Seasons of Human Nature* (Big Pine, CA: Lost Borders Press, 1998), and *The Roaring of the Sacred River* (Big Pine, CA: Lost Borders Press, 1989).

"Basic trust" is from Erik Erikson, *Identity and the Life Cycle* (New York: W.W. Norton & Company, 1980), 57.

Mircea Eliade, *Rites and Symbols of Initiation: The Mysteries of Birth and Rebirth* (Dallas, TX: Spring Publications, 1994), 112.

"hollow bone" is from Thomas E. Mails, *Fools Crow: Wisdom and Power* (Tulsa, OK: Council Oak Books, 1991).

We are children of the sun... From a workshop with Victor Sanchez, a passionate exponent of the teachings of indigenous peoples of Mexico who still follow the Toltec way of knowledge. See bibliography for a listing of his books.

"I am blind and do not see the things of this world..." is from *Indian Spirit*, edited by Michael Oren Fitzgerald (World Wisdom, Inc., 2003), 5.

The author has undertaken everything to ascertain that the copyright for quoted material has been observed and gratefully acknowledges all permissions given. Should anyone have been inadvertently overlooked please contact the author.

BIBLIOGRAPHY

All the texts listed here are not cited in this book. I have included works that have helped shape the narrative in one way or another.

Adyashanti. *The End of Your World.* Boulder, CO: Sounds True, 2008.

Andrews, Ted. *Animal Speaks.* St. Paul, MN: Llewellyn Publications, 1998.

Avens, Robert. *The New Gnosis.* Dallas, TX: Spring Publications, 1984

Batchelor, Stephen. *Buddhism Without Beliefs: A Contemporary Guide to Awakening.* New York: Riverhead Books, 1997. *Living with the Devil: A Meditation on Good and Evil.* New York: Riverhead Books, 2004.

Berry, Thomas. *The Great Work: Our Way into the Future.* New York: Bell Tower, 1999.

Black Elk, Nicholas. *Black Elk Speaks, as told through John G. Neihardt (Flaming Rainbow).* Lincoln, Nebraska: University of Nebraska Press, 2002.

Bly, Robert, ed. *Selected Poems of Rainer Maria Rilke.* New York: Harper & Row, 1981. *Iron John.* Reading, MA: Addison-Wesley, 1990. *The Sibling Society.* New York: Vintage Books, 1996. *The Kabir Book, Forty-Four of the Ecstatic Poems of Kabir.* Seventies Press, 1977. Reprinted by permission of Beacon Press, Boston.

Bly, Robert, James Hillman, and Michael Meade, eds. *The Rag and Bone Shop of the Heart.* New York: HarperCollins, 1992.

Bookchin, Murray. *Remaking Society.* Montreal: Black Rose, 1989.

Borgmann, Albert. *Crossing the Postmodern Divide.* Chicago: University of Chicago Press, 1992.

Brach, Tara. *Radical Acceptance: Embracing Your Life with the Heart of a Buddha.* New York: Bantam Books, 2003.

Brown, Joseph Epes, ed., *The Sacred Pipe: Black Elk's Account of the Seven Sacred Rites Of the Oglala Sioux.* Norman, OK: University of Oklahoma Press, 1989.

Bruchac, Joseph. *Native American Stories: Told by Joseph Bruchac.* Golden, CO: Fulcrum Publishing, 1991.

Campbell, Joseph. *The Hero with a Thousand Faces.* Princeton, NJ: Princeton University Press, 1968. *Myths to Live By.* New York: Arkana, 1993.

Camus, Albert. *The Rebel: An Essay on Man in Revolt,* trans. Anthony Bower. New York: Knopf Publishing Group, 1956.

Carlson, Kathie. *Life's Daughter/Death's Bride: Inner Transformation Through the Goddess Demeter/Persephone.* Boston: Shambhala, 1997.

Chatwin, Bruce. *The Songlines.* New York: Penquin Books, 1987.

Chodron, Pema. *The Wisdom of No Escape and the Path of Loving-Kindness.* Boston: Shambhala, 1991. *When Things Fall Apart: Heart Advice for Difficult Times.* Boston: Shambhala, 1997. *Tonglen: The Path of Transformation.* Halifax: Nova Scotia, Vajradhatu Publications, 2001. *No Time to Lose: A Timely Guide to the Way of the Bodhisattva.* Boston: Shambhala Publications, 2005.

Cousineau, Phil, ed. *The Hero's Journey: Joseph Campbell on his Life and Work.* Novato, CA: New World Library, 2003.

Cowan, Tom. *Fire in the Head: Shamanism and the Celtic Spirit.* San Francisco: Harper SanFrancisco, 1993.

Dalai Lama, His Holiness and Howard C. Cutler. *The Art of Happiness: A Handbook for Living.* New York: Riverhead Books, 1998.

Dreamer, Oriah Mountain. *The Invitation.* New York: HarperCollins Publishers, 1999.

Edinger, Edward F. *Anatomy of the Psyche: Alchemical Symbolism in Psychotherapy.* La Salle, Ill: Open Court, 1988.

Eliade, Mircea. *Cosmos and History: The Myth of the Eternal Return.* New York: Harper & Rowe, 1959. *Rites and Symbols of Initiation: The Mysteries of Birth and Rebirth.* Dallas, TX: Spring Publications, 1994.

Erikson, Erik. *Identity and the Life Cycle.* New York: W.W. Norton & Company, 1980.

Estes, Clarissa Pinkola. *Women Who Run with the Wolves: Myths and Stories of the Wild Woman Archetype.* New York: Ballantine Books, 1992.

Fisher, Andy. *Radical Ecopsychology: Psychology in the Service of Life.* Albany, NY: State University of New York Press, 2002.

Fitzgerald, Michael Oren, ed. *Indian Spirit.* Bloomington, IN: World Wisdom, Inc., 2003.

Foster, Steven and Little, Meredith. *The Roaring of the Sacred River: The Wilderness Quest for Vision and Self-Healing.* Big Pine, CA: Lost Borders Press, 1989. *The Four Shields: The Initiatory Seasons of Human Nature.* Big Pine, CA: Lost Borders Press, 1998.

Gimbutas, Marija. *The Goddesses and Gods of Old Europe – 6500-3500 b.c.,* Berkeley & Los Angeles: University of California Press, 1982.

Glendinning, Chellis. *"My Name is Chellis & I'm in Recovery from Western Civilization."* Boston: Shambhala Publications, 1994.

Hanh, Thich Nhat. *Being Peace.* Berkeley, CA: Parallax Press, 1987.

Heidegger, Martin. *Being and Time,* trans. by John Macquarrie & Edward Robinson, New York: Harper & Row, 1962.

Henderson, Joseph L.. *Thresholds of Initiation.* Middletown, CT: Wesleyan University Press, 1967.

Hillman, James. *"Anima Mundi: The Return of the Soul to the World."* New Orleans, LA: Spring Journal, 1982.

Hillman, James. *Re-Visioning Psychology.* New York: Harper Perennial, 1992.

Hull, Fritz, ed. *Earth & Spirit: The Spiritual Dimension of the Environmental Crisis.* New York: Continuum, 1993.

Jeffers, Robinson. *The Collected Poems of Robinson Jeffers, Volume 1,* Edited by Tim Hunt. La Jolla, CA: Stanford University Press, 2005.

Johnson, Robert. *He: Understanding Masculine Psychology.* New York: Harper & Row, 1974.

Johnson, Flynn. "Exploring Second Nature: Youth, Wilderness, & Rites of Initiation," *EarthLight: The Magazine of Spiritual Ecology,* Winter 2002/Issue 4. A version of this chapter first appeared in the above.

Jung, Carl G. *The Archetypes and the Collective Unconscious,* trans. R.F.C. Hull. Princeton University Press, 1980. *Modern Man in Search of a Soul.* Abingdon, Oxon, UK: Routledge, 2005. *Mysterium Coniunctionis: An Inquiry into the Separation and Synthesis of Psychic Opposites in Alchemy,* trans. R.F.C. Hull. Princeton, NJ: Princeton University Press, 1977.

Keeney, Bradford. *Shaking out the Spirits: A Psychotherapist's Entry into the Healing Mysteries of Global Shamanism.* Barrytown, NY: Station Hill Press, 1994.

Korten, David C. *The Great Turning: From Empire to Earth Community.* San Francisco: Berrett-Koehler Publishers, and Bloomfield, CT: Kumarian Press, 2006.